Class Actions in Privacy Law

Class actions in privacy law are rapidly growing as a legal vehicle for citizens around the world to hold corporations liable for privacy violations. Current and future developments in these class actions stand to shift the corporate liability landscape for companies that interact with people's personal information.

Privacy class actions are at the intersection of civil litigation, privacy law, and data protection. Developments in privacy class actions raise complex issues of substantive law as well as challenges to the established procedures governing class action litigation. Their outcomes are already integral to the evolution of privacy law and data protection law across jurisdictions. This book brings together established scholars in privacy law, data protection law, and collective litigation to offer a detailed perspective on the present and future of collective litigation for privacy claims.

Taking a comparative approach, this book incorporates considerations from consumer protection law, procedural law, cross-border litigation, tort law, and data protection law, which are key to understanding the development of privacy class actions. In doing so, it offers an analysis of the novel challenges they pose for courts, regulatory agencies, scholars, and litigators, together with their potential solutions.

Ignacio N. Cofone is an assistant professor and Norton Rose Fulbright Faculty Scholar at McGill University Faculty of Law.

Class Actions in Privacy Law

Edited by Ignacio N. Cofone

Routledge
Taylor & Francis Group

LONDON AND NEW YORK

First published 2021
by Routledge
2 Park Square, Milton Park, Abingdon, Oxon OX14 4RN

and by Routledge
52 Vanderbilt Avenue, New York, NY 10017

Routledge is an imprint of the Taylor & Francis Group, an informa business

British Library Cataloguing-in-Publication Data
A catalogue record for this book is available from the British Library

Library of Congress Cataloging-in-Publication Data
A catalog record for this book has been requested

ISBN: 978-0-367-50862-3 (hbk)
ISBN: 978-0-367-61730-1 (pbk)
ISBN: 978-1-003-08051-0 (ebk)

Typeset in Times New Roman
by Apex CoVantage, LLC

Contents

List of contributors   viii
Acknowledgements   ix

1 Introduction to privacy class actions   1
IGNACIO N. COFONE

   1 Introduction 1
   2 The importance of class actions for people's privacy 2
   3 Privacy's fit in class action claims 4
   4 Legal pathways for privacy class actions 6
   5 This book: common themes 9
   6 Roadmap 10

2 Privacy class actions' unfulfilled promise   13
JOHN J.A. LENZ

   1 Introduction 13
   2 Overview of class actions law 14
      a What is a class action? 14
      b Class actions legislation 15
      c The three advantages of class actions 17
   3 Privacy class actions: marriage or mismatch? 18
      *a Expected application of class actions to privacy
         claims 18*
      *b Practical application of class actions to privacy
         claims 20*
      c Concluding thoughts on this section 23

4 Towards more widespread use of privacy class actions 23
   a Cause of action: damages may not be
     "compensable" 24
   b Commonality: privacy's inherent individuality? 25
   c Representation: business incentives of plaintiff-side
     class actions lawyers 27
   d (Re)definition: more widespread accessibility of the
     privacy class action 28
5 Conclusion 29

**3 Uncertainties and Lessons Learned from Data
Protection Laws**   **30**
ELOISE GRATTON AND LAUREN PHIZICKY

1 Introduction 30
2 Privacy wrongdoing 33
   a Data security incidents 35
   b Intrusive business model 39
3 Damages 43
   a Subjective harm 43
   b Objective harm 47
4 Conclusion 53

4 *Douez v Facebook* and privacy class actions   **56**
JANET WALKER

1 Introduction 56
2 Sponsored stories: "there oughta be a law . . ." 57
   a Facebook goes to Ottawa 57
   b Two missed opportunities 58
3 Consumer contracts are different 60
   a A law without grammar 60
   b Safeguarding consumers' rights, promoting certainty
     for businesses 62
4 Privacy class actions: changing times 64
   a Inequality of bargaining power and class actions 64
   b Privacy class actions in the digital era 66
5 Quasi-constitutional rights and mandatory law 67
   a The real culprit revealed: PIPA 68
   b Mandatory rules vs. public policy 70
   c Mandatory rules and questions of procedure 72

6 *The limits of comity 73*
   a *Parallel proceedings with different equities and policy concerns 73*
   b *Claiming BC privacy rights in California 75*
7 Morguard *in a post-territorial world 78*

5 **Why class action suits for security breaches need to look beyond privacy concerns** 81
NICOLAS VERMEYS

   1 *Introduction 81*
   2 *Security breaches as a legal construct 83*
      a *What is information security? 83*
      b *The limits of security breach notification legislation 86*
   3 *Security breaches as a premise for class action suits 90*
      a *The problem with class action suits for security breaches 90*
      b *How to rethink security breach liability 96*
   4 *Conclusion 98*

6 *Cy près* **settlements in privacy class actions** 99
THOMAS E. KADRI AND IGNACIO N. COFONE

   1 *Introduction 99*
   2 Cy près *in* Frank v. Gaos *101*
   3 *The particular usefulness of* cy près *for privacy class actions 105*
   4 *The challenges of implementing* cy près *107*
   5 *Implementing* cy près *in a bijural Canada 109*
   6 *Conclusion 112*

Bibliography 113
Index 127

Contributors

Ignacio N. Cofone is an assistant professor and Norton Rose Fulbright Faculty Scholar at McGill University, Faculty of Law.

Eloïse Gratton is a partner at Borden Ladner Gervais, LLP and adjunct professor at University of Montreal, Faculty of Law.

Thomas E. Kadri is an assistant professor at the University of Georgia School of Law.

John J.A. Lenz is an articling student at Blake, Cassels & Graydon, LLP.

Lauren Phizicky is an attorney at Borden Ladner Gervais, LLP.

Nicolas Vermeys is a professor at the University of Montreal Faculty of Law and associate director of the University of Montreal's Cyberjustice Laboratory.

Janet Walker is a professor and former associate dean at Osgoode Hall Law School.

Acknowledgements

This book started out of academic exchanges between participants at the *Privacy Revolution* conference in 2019. I'm grateful to the Centre for Intellectual Property Policy at McGill University, which provided the framework for the event and this book, and its director Pierre-Emmanuel Moyse. I also acknowledge the generous support of the Caroline Bérubé and Jean Gabriel Castel funds at McGill University. More broadly, I'm grateful for the institutional support of the Faculty of Law and its Dean Robert Leckey. A special mention is owed to ten anonymous peer reviewers who provided feedback for each chapter and the book as a whole. Most importantly, five stellar McGill law students and research assistants, Francis Langlois, Cédrick Mulcair, Malaya Powers, Ana Qarri, and Catalina Turriago, provided invaluable help at every stage.

1 Introduction to privacy class actions

Ignacio N. Cofone

1 Introduction

Privacy class actions are a fast-growing phenomenon at the intersection of civil litigation, privacy, and data protection. Developments in privacy class actions are set to shift the corporate liability landscape for companies that interact with information technology and personal information and change how people seek redress for privacy violations. This book aims to fill a gap in the legal literature by being the first dedicated exclusively to the burgeoning phenomenon of class actions in privacy law.

Although privacy class actions are new, they are rapidly developing, with their numbers having surged since 2015.[1] In the coming years, the role of privacy class actions as a legal vehicle for citizens around the world to hold corporations accountable for privacy breaches and violations is likely to continue to grow. With the ubiquitous use of networked technologies across industries, the collection of and access to citizens' and consumers' personal information have become commonplace. Breach notification legislation, along with recent developments in privacy tort law in the United States and Canada,[2] have contributed to an explosion in privacy class actions. Public and private bodies are therefore increasingly at risk of liability for privacy

---

1 See Eloïse Gratton & Lauren Phizicky, "Privacy Class Actions: Uncertainties and lessons learned from data protection laws" (Chapter 3).

2 For a summary of recent developments in U.S. and Canadian privacy tort law, see generally Scott Skinner-Thomson, "Privacy's Double Standard" (2018) 93:4 Wash L Rev 2051 (U.S.); Ignacio N Cofone & Adriana Z Robertson, "Privacy Harms" (2018) 69 Hastings LJ 1039 (U.S.); Justin Safayeni, "Invasions of Privacy: Civil and Regulatory Consequences" in Gerald Chan & Nader R Hasan, eds, *Digital Privacy: Criminal, Civil and Regulatory Litigation* (Toronto: LexisNexis, 2018) at 183 (Can.); Leon Trakman, Robert Walters & Bruno Zeller, "Tort and Data Protection Law: Are There Any Lessons to be Learnt?" (2019) 5:4 European Data Protection L Rev 500.

breaches and violations, whether due to their business practices or external reasons such as hacking.

Developments in privacy class actions raise issues of both substantive and procedural law. They force us to challenge aspects of, for example, torts and consumer law, as well as the traditional procedures governing class action litigation. A study of privacy class actions such as this one therefore necessarily pulls together different branches of law, such as consumer protection, civil procedure, cross-border litigation, tort law, and data protection law. For that reason, this book brings together scholars from various fields to offer different perspectives on collective litigation for privacy claims.

The outcomes of ongoing and future cases stand to be integral to the evolution of privacy and data protection law across jurisdictions. Despite the increasing rate at which new privacy class actions are filed every year and their economic importance for consumers, public entities, and corporations, legal literature on the topic is scarce. This book aims to contribute to the development of this emerging area of the law.

2 The importance of class actions for people's privacy

Private rights of action are a key legal tool for citizen and consumer data protection.[3] As Mark Rotenberg and David Jacobs note:

> The enforcement of rights is a critical requirement of privacy law. Absent actual enforcement, there is little meaningful incentive for companies to comply with privacy requirements. Enforcement also helps to ensure that the individuals whose privacy is placed at risk are fairly compensated.[4]

Starting a claim under Canada's Personal Information Protection and Electronic Documents Act (PIPEDA), for example, is a long and arduous process. Individuals must first report the privacy-violating practice to the Office of the Canada Privacy Commissioner (OPC) or, depending on the

---

3 See Janet Walker, "Douez v Facebook and Privacy Class Actions" (Chapter 4); Ignacio N Cofone, "Privacy Law Needs Privacy Harm" (August 30, 2019), online: *The Hill* <thehill. com/opinion/cybersecurity/459427-privacy-law-needs-privacy-harm>.

4 Mark Rotenberg & David Jacobs, "Enforcing Privacy Rights: Class Action Litigation and the Challenge of *cy pres*" in David Wright & Paul De Hert, eds, *Enforcing Privacy: Regulatory, Legal and Technological Approaches* (Switzerland: Springer, 2016) 307 at 307.

type of entity and violation, a provincial privacy commissioner, and wait for the commissioner to investigate and release a report of findings. Then, they may start a *de novo* application in court pursuant to section 14 of PIPEDA within a year after the OPC has published its report of findings stating that the company has breached PIPEDA. This means there rarely is a cost-effective option in Canada for individuals to bring consumer privacy claims that will grant them redress.

Private rights of action in privacy law, in turn, are of limited use if they cannot be part of a mechanism of collective redress because of their small expected awards coupled with the costs of litigation. For example, in Ontario, privacy claims under the intrusion upon seclusion tort created by the landmark case *Jones v. Tsige* would result in small awards because of the established maximum of $20,000 in damages.[5] Many individual privacy claims involve much smaller amounts,[6] are difficult to quantify,[7] or go unrecognized.[8] In most cases, plaintiffs obtain much less, meaning that most people simply will not commence these claims individually.[9]

Moreover, most of these individual claims would be litigated in small claims courts, many of which do not keep records of their decisions. For example, the Ontario Small Claims Court has jurisdiction for claims up to $35,000 so, under the *Jones* cap, it would receive most privacy claims, unless they are coupled with punitive damages or contractual breach damages.[10] This impedes the development of privacy law.[11]

The need for a cost-effective mechanism that provides redress for privacy violations has made privacy class actions highly relevant to judges, corporations, consumers, and citizens in general. Consequently, there has been a remarkable upward trend in the number of privacy class actions over time. Canada, for example, has seen more than 80 privacy class actions in the past 10 years distributed in logarithmic growth, compared to

---

5 *Jones v. Tsige*, 2012 ONCA 32 [*Jones*].

6 See Ignacio N Cofone & Thomas Kadri, "*Cy Près* Settlements in Privacy Class Actions" (Chapter 6).

7 Ignacio N Cofone, "The Dynamic Effect of Information Privacy Law" (2017) 18:2 Minn J L Sci & Tech 517; Ignacio N Cofone, "A Healthy Amount of Privacy: Quantifying Privacy Concerns in Medicine" (2017) 65:1 Clev St L Rev 1.

8 Ignacio N Cofone, "Nothing to Hide, But Something to Lose" (2019) 70:1 UTLJ 64.

9 See Cofone & Kadri, *supra* note 6.

10 See "Privacy Law Update: Jones v. Tsige" (April 2, 2012), online: *Nelligan Law* <nelliganlaw. ca/article/insurance-defence/privacy-law-update-jones-v-tsige/>; "Small Claims Court" (last modified March 28, 2020), online: *Ministry of Attorney General*

11 See John JA Lenz, "Privacy Class Actions' Unfulfilled Promise" (Chapter 2).

only 2 commenced before 2010.[12] While the majority of them have been filed in Ontario using *Jones* as a catalyzer, they have spread across Canadian provinces widely.[13]

What these class actions have in common is that they stem from privacy violations. Different types of privacy violations give rise to private rights of action that can lead to privacy class actions. Privacy law protects the collection, processing, and dissemination of personal information, and violations at any of these three stages can give rise to class actions when formal requirements are met. Common examples of violations include: security breaches, either as a cybersecurity breach or unauthorized access to devices that hold personal information;[14] lack of notification when there's a statutory notification requirement;[15] unauthorized disclosure of personal information;[16] unauthorized collection of personal information;[17] and misuse of personal information.[18]

3 Privacy's fit in class action claims

Class proceedings are one of the foundational blocks of privacy class actions. Legislation enabled class proceedings in Quebec in 1978 and Ontario in 1992 – the first common law province to enact class proceedings legislation.[19] Since then, class proceedings have become a developing area of procedural law in Canada. New cases continue to shape the requirements for certification in Ontario and authorization in Quebec.[20]

---

12 Christopher Naudie & Evan Thomas, "Privacy Class Actions, by the Numbers" (May 31, 2017), online (blog): *Osler* <osler.com/en/blogs/classactions/may-2017/privacy-class-actions-by-the-numbers>.

13 See Gratton & Phizicky, *supra* note 1.

14 See e.g. *Agnew-Americano v Equifax Canada Co*, 2018 ONSC 275.

15 See e.g. *Antman v Uber Technologies, Inc*, 2018 WL 2151231 (ND Cal 2018). This claim alleged that Uber failed to notify its drivers of a security breach that compromised their personal information, violating notification requirements set out in the Civil Code of California.

16 See e.g. *Frank v Gaos*, 139 S Ct 1041 (2019).

17 See e.g. *Douez v Facebook, Inc*, 2018 BCCA 186.

18 See e.g. Carlo Di Carlo, "Invasions of Privacy: Class Proceedings" in Gerald Chan & Nader R Hasan, eds, *Digital Privacy: Criminal, Civil and Regulatory Litigation* (Toronto: LexisNexis, 2018) at 246, citing *Simpson v Facebook, Inc*, ONSC File No. CV-18-00597085-00CP. The class proceeding alleged that Facebook gave Cambridge Analytica access to the personal information of 620,000 Canadians.

19 Janet Walker et al, *Class Actions in Canada: Cases, Notes, and Materials*, 2nd ed (Toronto: Emond Publishing, 2018) at 21.

20 *Ibid* at 37–98.

One of the policy goals of introducing class proceedings in Canadian procedural law was to increase access to justice.[21] Nonetheless, the degree to which this goal has been realized continues to be debated in class actions literature. Some argue that, although class actions are touted as a success story of Canadian access to justice reform, "the notion that class actions inevitably open the doors to justice is unsupportable."[22] Although class actions increase the number and types of claims that can be litigated, their success in providing a fair and proper remedy for injuries suffered by a class is contested.

This idea is patent in privacy class actions. One of the major benefits of bringing privacy claims through class actions is their affordability for class members. Usually, there is no upfront cost for class members. This is of particular importance in privacy claims, where the remedy is of uncertain success and is likely to be low if successful. At the same time, to be effective at increasing access to justice, privacy class actions must overcome obstacles stemming from privacy law, such as the difficulty in proving privacy harm, and obstacles stemming from procedural law, such as class certification.

Class actions in privacy law also face issues of multijurisdictional and cross-border claims. Many class actions in privacy law are extraterritorial by nature. Despite uncertainties about the constitutionality of interprovincial claims in Canada, courts have certified them since the early days of class proceedings.[23] For that reason, comparative work is particularly important for privacy class actions. Scholarship in approaches to damages, injunctions, and other remedies for breach of privacy from a comparative perspective,[24] as well as studies on the challenges faced by courts as they determine appropriate and fair remedies,[25] are directly relevant for drawing attention to how privacy class actions provide insights into substantive law. Canada, in turn, is an interesting case study for comparative work on the topic, as it combines common law and civil law jurisdictions, which often take different approaches to protecting individual interests as a matter of private law, holding lessons for a wide number of jurisdictions.

Privacy class actions have been classified in three types depending on the type of wrongdoing that led to the class action claim: (a) hacker-based

---

21 The Supreme Court of Canada recognized this as one of the three objectives of class actions. See Walker et al, *supra* note 19 at 11.
22 Jasminka Kalajdzic, *Class Actions in Canada: The Promise and Reality of Access to Justice* (Vancouver: UBC Press, 2019).
23 Walker et al, *supra* note 19 at 239.
24 Jason Varuhas & NA Moreham, *Remedies for Breach of Privacy* (London: Hart Publishing, 2018).
25 *Ibid.*

claims; (b) business models that infringe privacy interests; and (c) mishaps, usually involving employee negligence or, more rarely, intentional acts.[26] As the next section explores, these class actions can arrive through different legal pathways.

4 Legal pathways for privacy class actions

Independent of the type of wrongdoing mentioned above, privacy class actions can emerge from three different legal pathways. The wrongs alleged in privacy class actions can be brought to court through (a) a violation of a consumer privacy statute,[27] (b) a security breach,[28] or (c) a privacy tort.[29] These legal pathways are not mutually exclusive.

Some consumer privacy and data protection statutes give rise to the first legal pathway: direct private rights of action when a statute is breached. Some notorious examples are Washington, D.C.'s Use of Consumer Identification Information Act[30] and Illinois' Biometric Information Privacy Act,[31] which famously triggered a lawsuit against Six Flags.[32] More recent examples are a class action lawsuit against Clearview AI for building one of the largest facial recognition databases in history[33] and a class action against Zoom for allegedly sharing data with Facebook.[34]

In Canada, a more indirect recourse exists. Federally, as mentioned above, individuals may make a *de novo* application after the OPC has published their report.[35] Similar causes of action exist in provinces that enacted private-sector privacy laws substantially similar to PIPEDA, such as Alberta, B.C., and Quebec.[36] Under the European General Data Protection

---

26 Di Carlo, *supra* note 18 at 237. See also Naudie & Thomas, *supra* note 12.
27 See e.g. *Rosenbach v Six Flags Entertainment Corp*, 129 NE (3d) 1197 (Ill Sup Ct 2019) [*Rosenbach v Six Flags*].
28 See e.g. *Lewert v P.F. Chang's China Bistro, Inc*, 819 F (3d) 963 (7th Cir 2016).
29 See e.g. *Broutzas v Rouge Valley Health System*, 2018 ONSC 6315.
30 See e.g. *Hancock v Urban Outfitters, Inc*, 830 F (3d) 511 (DC Cir 2016).
31 *Biometric Information Privacy Act*, 740 Ill Comp Stat 14/1.
32 See e.g. *Rosenbach v Six Flags, supra* note 27.
33 Complaint, David Mutnick v Clearview AI, Inc, No 1:20-cv-00512 (ND Ill January 22, 2020).
34 Isobel Asher Hamilton, "Zoom Is Being Sued for Allegedly Handing Over Data to Facebook" (March 31, 2020), online: *Business Insider* <businessinsider.com/zoom-sued-allegedly-sharing-data-with-facebook-2020-3>.
35 Michael Power, *The Law of Privacy*, 2nd ed (Toronto: LexisNexis, 2017) at 188.
36 *Personal Information Protection Act*, SA 2003, c P-6.5, s 60; *Personal Information Protection Act*, SBC 2003, c 63, s 57; Karl Delwaide & Antoine Aylwin, *Learning from a Decade*

Regulation (GDPR), on the other hand, there is some case law on private rights of action stemming directly from loss of control produced by behavior that breached GDPR under art. 82(1),[37] without the need for a prior declaration from a data protection authority, but these are an exception and enforcement is mainly public by national data protection authorities.[38]

Security breaches are the second legal pathway to privacy class actions. These breaches are a "voluntary or accidental attempt to affect the confidentiality, integrity or availability of data or data systems."[39] Most commonly, these are insufficient protections for hacking incidents violating a cybersecurity statute or lack of notification for a data breach. Notably, the GDPR and PIPEDA have made breach notifications to affected individuals mandatory, leading to accessible privacy class action claims.[40] So do some provincial statutes in Canada, such as the Act to Establish a Legal Framework for Information Technology in Quebec.[41] Similarly, the California Consumer Privacy Act creates civil penalties and a private right of action for violations of the statute that give consumers some ability to bring a civil suit for actual

---

of Experience: Quebec's Private Sector Privacy Act (Ottawa: Privacy Commissioner of Canada, 2005) at 35.

37 Rechtbank Overijssel [Overijssel District Court], Zwolle, May 28, 2019, AWB 18/2047 (Netherlands) (de Rechtspraak). DLA Piper, "Germany: First Court Decision on Claims for Immaterial Damages under GDPR" (December 12, 2018), online (blog): *Privacy Matters* <blogs.dlapiper.com/privacymatters/germany-first-court-decision-on-claims-for-immaterial-damages-under-gdpr/>.

38 See Gabriela Zanfir-Fortuna, "Article 82" in Christopher Kuner, Lee A Bygrave & Christopher Docksey, eds, *The EU General Data Protection Regulation: A Commentary* (Oxford: Oxford University Press, 2020); EC, *Regulation (EU) 2016/679 of 27 April 2016 on the protection of natural persons with regard to the processing of personal data and on the free movement of such data, and repealing Directive 95/46/ EC (General Data Protection Regulation)*, [2016] OJ, L 119/1 [GDPR] arts 79, 82(1).

39 Nicolas Vermeys, "Why Class Action Suits for Security Breaches Need to Look Beyond Privacy Concerns" (Chapter 5) at 6.

40 See generally Andrae J Marrocco, Lyndsay Wasser & Mitch Koczerginski, "Data Protection and Cybersecurity in Canada" (2019) 39:1 Franchise LJ 81; Stephen D Burns et al, "Breach Notification Rules Under GDPR, PIPEDA, and PIPA" (October 1, 2018), online (blog): *Bennett Jones* <bennettjones.com/Blogs-Section/Breach-Notification-Rules-under-GDPR-PIPEDA-and-PIPA>. See also GDPR, *supra* note 38, arts 33–34 on notification requirements for personal data breaches and *Personal Information Protection and Electronic Documents Act*, SC 2000, c 5, ss 10.1(1) – 10.3(2), Division 1.1 "Breaches of Security Safeguards". PIPEDA, however, has a narrow approach that limits these to security breaches of personal information (leaving aside other types of data) and requiring the existence of a risk of harm, limiting the eventual legal recourse of victims of violations of other types of data. See Ibid at 9.

41 Act to *Establish a Legal Framework* for Information Technology, CQLR c C-1.1, s 25.

or statutory damages, whichever is greater, for claims related to data security breaches.[42] As a result, several class action suits in the United States and Canada have been triggered by security breaches.[43]

Privacy torts are the third legal pathway that can trigger a privacy class action. Some Canadian provinces, like Ontario, have common law privacy torts, and five provinces have statutorily created privacy torts with their own causes of action.[44] In British Columbia, Saskatchewan, Manitoba, and Newfoundland and Labrador, privacy statutes create the tort of "violation of privacy" for disputes between private citizens; these claims are actionable without proof of damage when their criteria are met.[45] In Quebec, the right to privacy is codified in articles 35 and 36 of the Civil Code of Quebec, which dictate that an individual's privacy may not be invaded without his or her consent and provides examples of what constitutes actionable privacy violations.[46]

In the United States, the privacy tort that can give rise to private rights of action is formed by intrusion upon seclusion, private disclosure of public facts, false light, and appropriation.[47] The most fitting for privacy class actions are intrusion upon seclusion and public disclosure of private facts, as they are the ones that involve privacy interests more directly.[48] Privacy literature in American and Canadian tort law recognizes the expansion of these claims, in the United States since Prosser's classification,[49] and in Canada since the introduction of the tort of intrusion upon seclusion in *Jones*.[50] In some European countries, similarly, privacy claims related to the

---

42 Anupam Chandler, Margot Kaminski & William McGeveran, "Catalyzing Privacy Law" [draft 2020] at 21; *California Consumer Privacy Act*, 1.81.5 Cal Civ Code § 1798.150, § 1798.155(a)-(b) (2018).

43 Vermeys, *supra* note 39, at 2.

44 B.C.: *Privacy Act*, RSBC 1996, c 373; Saskatchewan: *Privacy Act*, RSS 1978, c P-24; Manitoba: *Privacy Act*, RSM 1987 c P-125; Newfoundland and Labrador: *Privacy Act*, RSN 1990, c P-22.

45 Power, *supra* note 35 at 221.

46 Arts 35–36 CCQ.

47 Daniel J Solove & Paul M Schwartz, *Privacy Law Fundamentals*, 5th ed (Portsmouth, NH: IAPP, 2019) at 2, 17–22.

48 Cofone & Robertson, *supra* note 2.

49 Solove & Schwartz, *supra* note 47.

50 See Barbara McIsaac, Kris Klein & Shaun Brown, *Privacy Law in Canada* (Toronto: Thomson Reuters Publishing, 2018) (addressing the regulation of the collection and use of personal information in Canada and, within it, identifying points that still require clarification in privacy torts case law); Jeffrey A. Kaufman, *Privacy Law in the Private Sector* (Toronto: Thomson Reuters Publishing, 2019) (discussing how privacy torts might continue to evolve in Canada through a comparative analysis). See also *Jones, supra* note 5.

GDPR have been successful through tort law, such as in The Netherlands under Article 6:106 of the Dutch Civil Code.[51]

A question that comes up in different jurisdictions is whether the existence of a publicly enforced statute pre-empts people from suing on the basis of the privacy tort when a business practice constitutes both a tort and a breach of a data protection or privacy statute. In Canada, this has been answered in the negative in *Jones*.[52] Similarly, in some civil law European Union countries, such as Germany, people can sue under tort law, referencing a GDPR violation as a law that protects individual rights.[53] The U.K. has also permitted different private rights of action without them being pre-empted by British data protection law.[54]

5 This book: common themes

This book addresses an underexplored intersection of privacy law and collective litigation. Together, its chapters explore three themes: the current trends in privacy class actions; the challenges related to identifying wrongdoing, fault, and harm in these claims; and their international nature.

The first theme is exploring trends in privacy class actions. The chapters document trends and developments in this area of civil litigation across jurisdictions, industries, and claims to date. The book begins by considering the fit between class actions and privacy claims. Chapters 2 and 3 theoretically and empirically examine the emergence of privacy class actions across Canada by documenting trends and developments in this area of civil litigation across provincial jurisdictions and industries. While privacy claims might, at first glance, seem like a natural fit for a procedural tool that aims to increase access to justice like class actions, the developing case law reveals a more complicated relationship, as does privacy claims' interaction with private-sector data protection frameworks.

---

51 See e.g. Overijssel District Court [Rechtbank Overijssel], May 28, 2019, AK_18_2047 (Netherlands), online: <uitspraken.rechtspraak.nl/inziendocument?id=ECLI:NL:RBOVE: 2019:1827>; Amsterdam District Court [Rechtbank Amsterdam], September 02, 2019, 7560515 CV EXPL 19–4611, online: <uitspraken.rechtspraak.nl/inziendocument?id=ECL I:NL:RBAMS:2019:6490>; North Holland District Court [Rechtbank Noord-Nederland], January 15, 2020, C/18/189406/HA ZA 19–6, online: <uitspraken.rechtspraak.nl/inziendo cument?id=ECLI:NL:RBNNE:2020:247>.
52 *Jones, supra* note 5 at paras 48–51.
53 Spindler/Horváth, "DS-GVO Art. 82 – Haftung und Recht auf Schadenersatz" in Spindler/ Schuster, eds, *Recht der elektronischen Medien*, 4th ed (Munich: CHBeck, 2019).
54 See "Halfords e-Receipt Service a Delivery System for Marketing" (May 6, 2018), online (blog): *Mind My Data* <mindmydata.co.uk/halfords-e-receipt-service-a-delivery-system-for-marketing/>.

The second theme is exploring privacy class actions' challenges. The challenges of identifying types of privacy wrongdoing and privacy harm and securing adequate remedy appear throughout the book. Some chapters explore how we might best understand and categorize the types of harms and wrongdoing implicated in privacy class action cases. While the success of privacy class actions at remedying privacy harms will become clearer as they continue to be heard on their merits, some chapters consider the ability of class actions to address privacy harms. These debates, which are present in privacy literature broadly, are acutely present in the context of class actions. These uncertainties affect the class certification process and, as Chapter 5 shows, security breaches as a basis for class action claims. Chapter 6 brings the conversation about conceptualizing privacy harms to the settlement stage of class actions by considering the *cy près* settlement tool as an alternative to individual compensation in class actions when damages are too diffuse or costly to distribute. These challenges affect privacy law and pose questions that scholars and professionals may consider as these class actions play out.

The third theme is the international nature of privacy class actions and the consequent usefulness of a comparative approach. While Chapters 2 and 3 offer a general framework for understanding the evolving role of class actions for privacy and data protection, the remaining chapters tackle specific issues. They focus on Canada with a comparative perspective, drawing on developments in different jurisdictions. Chapters 4 and 6, in particular, point to the international nature of this area of litigation. Privacy law is extraterritorial by nature, as many of the organizations implicated in class actions are international. National privacy laws are applied extraterritorially more than any other body of law because the sources and perpetrators of online harms are routinely in a different jurisdiction than their victim, so data protection regulations would be ineffective if they did not provide some protection from them. As seen in *Douez v. Facebook*,[55] privacy class actions have and will continue to raise questions at the intersection of privacy law and conflict of laws.

6 Roadmap

The rest of the book proceeds as follows.

In Chapter 2, John J.A. Lenz identifies and analyzes the specific obstacles hindering class actions' widespread use as a means to enforce privacy rights. Lenz argues that the purported advantages of class actions appear

---

55 *Douez v Facebook, Inc*, 2017 SCC 33.

to overcome many of the procedural difficulties associated with individual private law enforcement of privacy rights. However, privacy class actions tend to arise only under specific factual scenarios. Due to difficulties with conceptualizing common privacy harms across a class of plaintiffs, privacy class actions have been certified mostly in only a limited number of fact scenarios: a violation of personal health information, hacking or loss of a physical memory device, and unauthorized employee access. As such, class actions fail at their promised objectives in the privacy law sphere. In particular, three factors restrict the more widespread use of class actions to enforce privacy rights: the underdevelopment of substantive privacy law, the inherent individuality associated with privacy harms, and the economic incentives of plaintiff-side class action lawyers. Finally, the chapter discusses one way forward that would facilitate privacy class actions: reconceptualizing privacy harm.

In Chapter 3, Eloïse Gratton and Lauren Phizicky present a thorough analysis of the emergence of privacy class actions in Canada. They explore trends in privacy class action litigation by classifying the types of incidents that give rise to privacy class actions, jurisdictions within Canada, and industries implicated. This will be the first academic work to date to provide an empirical analysis of trends in privacy class action litigation in Canada. Further, the chapter undertakes a theoretical analysis of the claims that give rise to privacy class actions. Privacy class actions are relatively new, and although the Ontario Court of Appeal recently created the tort of "intrusion upon seclusion" in *Jones*, that decision may not apply throughout Canada. Furthermore, privacy torts are not a good fit for the types of claims that we are seeing, which stem primarily from mismanagement of personal information rather than activities such as eavesdropping or spying. This chapter assesses the wrongdoings and types of harm at stake through the lens of what is expected of organizations under Canada's data protection laws.

In Chapter 4, Janet Walker shows how the Supreme Court of Canada decision in the *Facebook* case highlighted many of the doctrinal issues to be tackled in the coming years and, in so doing, serves as a good illustration of what might lie ahead in the field of privacy class actions, and more generally, in the field of cross-border litigation. Particularly, the chapter analyzes three elements: (a) the protection of vulnerable classes of litigants from waiver of access to the local courts and the relevance of the practical difficulties that they might face in litigating in distant courts; (b) the need to recognize the role of mandatory rules in addition to the doctrine of public policy; and (c) whether the role of courts in regulating businesses operating in the digital economy needs to be reconsidered.

In Chapter 5, Nicolas Vermeys shows that, by limiting security breach notification requirements to a privacy issue, legislators have narrowed the scope of possible claims and the chances of success of class action suits based on these claims. In the absence of legislative will to address this issue, lawyers should reconsider their approach to security breach liability issues. Legal responses to security breaches address only their impact on personal information, and therefore limit the ability of those affected to seek recourse beyond privacy claims. Further, even within these claims, such an approach places unattainable evidentiary burdens on plaintiffs. They often face difficulties proving compensable privacy harms and establishing causality and, as a result, are unable to meet the certification threshold. A broader approach to security breaches that focuses on all elements of the AIC (availability, integrity, and confidentiality) triad – and moves beyond privacy – can strengthen and broaden the range of legal options for victims of security breaches.

In Chapter 6, Thomas E. Kadri and I consider the potential for using *cy près* settlements in privacy class actions. These settlements are a procedural mechanism that can be used to overcome distribution challenges in class actions. When it is too burdensome to prove individual claims or too costly to distribute damages to class members, courts on occasion award damages to a charity or nonprofit organization involved in work serving the class members' interests. These controversial settlements have been gaining attention in various legal systems. The U.S. Supreme Court recently considered their propriety in *Frank v. Gaos*, while courts in Canada and several Latin American countries have been experimenting with *cy près* as well. The chapter uses these cases to explore how this procedural mechanism can be particularly useful in privacy class actions. While *cy près* settlements require proper judicial supervision to prevent abuse, the chapter concludes that they can help to deter privacy invasions, enforce privacy laws, and provide plaintiffs with some measure of indirect relief when those laws are violated.

In such a way, this book intends to further the understanding of privacy class actions as a legal tool available to victims of privacy-related wrongdoing. Based on the topics covered in the chapters, this book aims to be useful to legal scholars, practicing lawyers, judges deciding on privacy class actions, and policymakers regulating the protection of personal information.

2 Privacy class actions' unfulfilled promise

John J.A. Lenz

1 Introduction

Privacy rights are important. Increasingly, jurists are attempting to conceptualize privacy and develop substantive legal mechanisms which promote the proper collection, use, and disclosure of personal information. Although private law mechanisms such as torts and statutory rights of action have been debated since the late nineteenth century,[1] the advent of the Internet and of social media (among other societal and technological changes) has brought new attention and perspectives to privacy law in Canada. Private law mechanisms allow a data subject to take direct action against the alleged wrongdoer by seeking relief and remedy from the courts.

The teeth of the private law, however, are dulled by a cumbersome procedure. Requiring individuals to go through a complex and expensive judicial system limits the pool of people who will be able to enforce their privacy rights. Furthermore, those who do go to court are rarely awarded enough compensation to make their efforts financially worthwhile. As a result, those who commit large-scale but individually modest privacy harms are seldom, if ever, held accountable for their wrongful conduct.

Without a suitable procedure to enforce one's privacy rights, they become illusory. The Supreme Court of Canada acknowledged that "[w]ithout an effective and accessible means of enforcing rights, the rule of law is threatened."[2] The class action is one such means. Class actions purport, among other advantages, to promote access to justice by lowering litigation costs for individual plaintiffs. "Without class actions, the doors of justice remain close to some plaintiffs, however strong their legal claims."[3] But

---

1 Samuel D Warren & Louis D Brandeis, "The Right to Privacy" (1890) 4:5 Harv L Rev 193.
2 *Hryniak v Mauldin*, 2014 SCC 7 at para 1.
3 *Western Canadian Shopping Centres Inc v Dutton*, 2001 SCC 46 at para 28 [*Dutton*].

despite its apparent appeal, class actions have only been applied to privacy cases under limited circumstances.

In light of these considerations, this chapter will identify and analyse obstacles hindering the class action's more widespread use as a means to enforce privacy rights in Canada. In the first section, I will provide an overview of class actions law in Canada, drawing attention to the differences between the law in Québec as compared to the common law jurisdictions. In the second section, I will first argue that the purported advantages of class actions appear to overcome many of the procedural difficulties associated with private law enforcement of privacy rights. I will then review the limited jurisprudence on privacy class actions, pointing out that they tend to arise only under specific factual scenarios. As such, class actions are not fulfilling their promised objectives in the privacy law sphere. In the third section, I will examine three factors restricting the more widespread use of class actions to enforce privacy rights: the underdevelopment of substantive privacy law, the inherent individuality associated with privacy harms, and the economic incentives of plaintiff-side class actions specialists. Finally, I will discuss one possible way forward that would facilitate privacy class actions.

2 Overview of class actions law

a What is a class action?

The class action is a procedural mechanism that enables one or more plaintiffs to bring an action on behalf of a group, or "class," of people. The class members' individual claims are aggregated and litigated once on a class-wide basis. As such, once a class action is decided on its merits, it permanently resolves the substantive rights of all class members. That is, a decision on the merits or a settlement precludes all individual class members from bringing subsequent claims on the same law and facts, since they would be bound as a matter of *res judicata* or issue estoppel.[4]

Judicial approval is required before a class proceeding can be tried on its merits. This approval is requested by way of a certification motion, or an authorization motion in Québec.[5] The certification motion must set out, *inter alia*, the class definition, which identifies those who will be bound

---

4 Warren K Winkler et al, *The Law of Class Actions in Canada* (Toronto: Thomson Reuters, 2014) at 1.

5 *Ibid* at 8; Shaun E Finn, *Class Actions in Québec: Notes for Non-Residents*, 2nd ed (Montréal: Thomson Reuters, 2018) at 1.

by the proceedings and name a representative plaintiff. Where certification (or authorization) is denied, individual claimants may still bring claims, although in many cases this will not be economically or practically possible.

b Class actions legislation

Legislation in ten Canadian jurisdictions sets out the conditions under which a class proceeding will be approved; the federal government and every province except for one have enacted class proceedings legislation.[6] Prince Edward Island remains the only jurisdiction without class actions legislation, although the province's Supreme Court recently allowed a class action to proceed despite this lack of legislation.[7]

The certification criteria at the federal level and in the common law provinces are nearly identical, whereas the Québec regime differs in several respects (which I will address at the end of this section). This chapter will use the Ontario Class Proceedings Act, 1992 (CPA) as illustrative of the common law frameworks.[8] This act establishes five certification criteria, which must all be met to grant certification.[9] The criteria are:

i Cause of action

Section 5(1)(a) of the CPA requires that "the pleadings or notice of application discloses a cause of action."[10] This criterion plays an important role in ensuring that claims which have no chance of success do not pass the certification stage. The representative plaintiff must plead all of the material facts needed to establish liability.[11] These facts must then be proven at the trial on the merits. Implicitly, this criterion further requires that the representative plaintiff's claim is not statute-barred.

ii Class definition

Section 5(1)(b) of the CPA demands "an identifiable class of two or more persons that would be represented by the representative plaintiff or defendant."[12] This requirement defines the scope of the class proceeding.

---

6 Winkler et al, *supra* note 4 at 1.
7 *King & Dawson v Government of PEI*, 2019 PESC 27.
8 *Class Proceedings Act, 1992*, SO 1992, c 6 [*CPA*].
9 *Ibid*, s 5.
10 *Ibid*, s 5(1)(a).
11 *Ragoonanan v Imperial Tobacco Canada Ltd*, 78 OR (3d) 98 at para 11, [2005] OJ No 4697.
12 *CPA*, *supra* note 8 at s 5(1)(b).

Class members must be able to determine whether or not they are members of the class based solely on the definition. Moreover, the class must be defined on the basis of objective factors such that class membership is not dependent on the merits of the action. For example, courts have rejected definitions formulated along the lines of "all persons who have suffered damages as a result of the defendant's conduct," because identifying those who will be bound by the class proceeding will be difficult until it is determined on the merits whether anyone has in fact suffered damages.[13]

iii Commonality

Section 5(1)(c) of the CPA mandates that "the claims or defences of the class members raise common issues."[14] The CPA defines a "common issue" essentially as a "common but not necessarily identical issue" of law or fact.[15] That is, there must be common issues whose resolution will avoid duplication of fact-finding or legal analysis and which can be answered independently of individual findings of fact.[16] Stated differently, the common issues must be "capable of being answered once for all class members."[17]

iv Preferability

Section 5(1)(d) bars certification unless "a class proceeding would be the preferable procedure for the resolution of the common issues."[18] Courts take a two-step approach to analysing the preferability requirement. First, "absolute preferability" asks whether a class proceeding would be a fair, efficient, and manageable method of advancing the claim. At this step, making smaller claims viable by spreading litigation costs across a large number of plaintiffs is a strong factor in favour of certification.[19] Second, "relative preferability" asks whether a class proceeding would be preferable to "all reasonably available means" of resolving the class members' claims, including both judicial and extrajudicial means.[20]

---

13 *Chadha v Bayer Inc*, 223 DLR (4th) 158 at para 69, 63 OR (3d) 22; *Bywater v Toronto Transit Commission*, 43 OR (3d) 367, [1999] OJ No 1402.

14 *CPA*, *supra* note 8 at s 5(1)(c).

15 *Ibid*, s 1.

16 *Dutton*, *supra* note 3 at para 39; *Fulawka v Bank of Nova Scotia*, 2012 ONCA 443 at para 81.

17 Winkler et al, *supra* note 4 at 112.

18 *CPA*, *supra* note 8 at s 5(1)(d).

19 Winkler et al, *supra* note 4 at 129.

20 *AIC Limited v Fischer*, 2013 SCC 69 at paras 19, 55 [*Fischer*].

v Adequacy of representation

The representative plaintiff must be a class member (that is, he or she must fall under the class definition) who "would fairly and adequately represent the interests of the class," has produced a "workable" litigation plan, and does not have an interest in conflict with the interests of the other class members on the common issues.[21] The representative plaintiff need not be "typical," nor be the "best possible representative," but rather should satisfy the court that he or she will "vigorously and capably prosecute the interests of the class."[22]

Québec's authorization criteria contrast with and are generally viewed as constituting a lower bar than their counterparts in common law Canada. Although there are similarities, the criteria are expressed in broader and more flexible terms, favouring authorization. In particular, courts adopt the approach that the common issues need not predominate over the individual issues, "even one common issue can be enough, provided that its resolution would be of benefit to each of the putative class members."[23] Furthermore, the preferability requirement is severely restricted; a class proceeding will be appropriate if it is "difficult or impracticable" to advance the claim by way of individual mandates or joinder.[24]

c The three advantages of class actions

In 2001, the Supreme Court of Canada delivered a trilogy of decisions which transformed the class actions landscape: *Western Canadian Shopping Centres Inc v Dutton*,[25] *Hollick v Toronto (City)*,[26] and *Rumley v British Columbia*.[27] All three unanimous decisions were penned by Chief Justice McLachlin. In *Dutton*, in a ubiquitously cited passage, she identified "three important advantages" which have formed the foundation of Canadian class actions law: judicial economy, access to justice, and behaviour modification.[28]

Class actions serve judicial economy by aggregating claims, thereby avoiding a multitude of similar proceedings. They free judicial resources and reduce litigation costs for both plaintiffs (who can share litigation costs) and defendants (who are only required to litigate once).[29]

21 *CPA, supra* note 8 at s 5(1)(e).
22 *Dutton, supra* note 3 at para 41.
23 Finn, *supra* note 5 at 19.
24 Art 575(3) CCP.
25 *Dutton, supra* note 3.
26 *Hollick v Toronto (City)*, 2001 SCC 68.
27 *Rumley v British Columbia*, 2001 SCC 69 [*Rumley*].
28 *Ibid* at paras 27–29.
29 *Ibid* at para 27.

Class actions purport to improve access to justice on several levels. In its most straightforward form, class actions open the court's doors to individuals to whom they would otherwise be closed by "making economical the prosecution of claims that would otherwise be too costly to prosecute individually."[30] This focus was expanded to include psychological or emotional barriers to access the courts in *Rumley*. That case was brought by survivors of sexual and other forms of abuse at a residential school for deaf and blind students. More recently, the Supreme Court turned its attention to procedural access to justice. It held that the plaintiffs' participation through the representative plaintiff "weighs heavily in favour" of the class action and that it was therefore preferable to an administrative proceeding.[31]

Class actions also strive to achieve behaviour modification. They help to ensure compliance with the substantive law by making it possible to pursue claims that could otherwise not be pursued individually. As such, class actions help deter perpetrators of "widespread but individually minimal harm."[32]

3 Privacy class actions: marriage or mismatch?

This section will explore the application of class actions law to privacy claims. I will first argue that, on the surface, the class action is a procedural tool well-suited to enforcing privacy rights, as the advantages of class actions seem to respond to many difficulties associated with bringing a privacy claim. The second part of this section will argue that, despite this theoretical alignment, privacy class actions only tend to arise if the case exhibits one or more of a limited number of factual attributes. As such, privacy claims and class actions should be a happy marriage, but in practice have been closer to a mismatch.

a Expected application of class actions to privacy claims

Before continuing, I must clarify what I refer to as a "privacy class action." While a precise definition of a "privacy harm," or for that matter even "privacy," continues to elude jurists,[33] certain private law statutory and common law causes of action are recognized as falling under the "privacy" umbrella. In particular, the Personal Information Protection and Electronic Documents

---

30 *Ibid* at para 28.
31 *Fischer, supra* note 20 at para 55.
32 *Dutton, supra* note 3 at para 29.
33 Ignacio N Cofone & Adriana Z Robertson, "Privacy Harms" (2018) 69 Hastings LJ 1039.

Act (PIPEDA) creates causes of action which regulate the collection, use, and disclosure of individuals' personal information by private-sector entities.[34] The Privacy Act has a similar objective for the public sector.[35] Additionally, in *Jones v Tsige*,[36] the Ontario Court of Appeal recognized the tort of intrusion upon seclusion. In November 2018, the Ontario Superior Court adopted another of Prosser's privacy torts, finding the defendants liable for "public disclosure of private facts."[37] In Québec, the Charter of Human Rights and Freedoms protects the "right to respect of [a person's] private life."[38] Moreover, in certain instances individuals can resort to the general civil liability provision in the Civil Code of Québec.[39]

Enforcing these privacy rights in the courts, however, is often complicated by inherent financial, institutional, and procedural difficulties. In particular, low damages awards, frequent steering towards small claims courts, and inappropriately tailored participatory obligations all reduce the ability of individuals to pursue all types of privacy claims.

At first glance, the advantages promised by class actions are well-suited to overcoming these obstacles.

First, privacy claims tend to attract a small measure of damages. Courts frequently treat injuries from privacy claims as injuries based on humiliation, embarrassment, or anxiety, rather than a *sui generis* type of injury.[40] Even when judges claim to account for the inherent economic value of the personal information, privacy cases tend to attract small damages awards, if any at all.[41] As a result, potential claimants may be hesitant or unable to seek recourse from the courts, as the potential compensation does not justify the cost and time needed to pursue the claim. Class actions respond to this concern. By spreading litigation costs across the class, a class proceeding makes it more economically feasible to bring a privacy claim.

Second, as the quantum of damages awarded is typically low, privacy claims risk being directed towards small claims courts.[42] There, plaintiffs have restricted access to legal representation and claimants are afforded

---

34 *Personal Information Protection and Electronic Documents Act*, SC 2000, c 5 at ss 3, 4(1) [*PIPEDA*].

35 *Privacy Act*, RSC 1985, c P-21.

36 *Jones v Tsige*, 2012 ONCA 32 [*Jones*].

37 *Jane Doe 72511 v Morgan*, 2018 ONSC 6607 at para 96 [*Jane Doe*].

38 *Charter of Human Rights and Freedoms*, CQLR c C-12 at s 5 [*QC Charter*].

39 Art 1457 CCQ.

40 See Finn, *supra* note 5.

41 Jessica L Hubley, "How *Concepcion* Killed the Privacy Class Action" (2011) 28:4 Santa Clara Comp & High Tech LJ 743 at 748.

42 Omar Ha-Redeye, "Class Action Intrusions: A Development in Privacy Rights or an Indeterminate Liability" (2015) 6 WJ Legal Stud 1 at 4.

less court time to present their case.[43] This is hardly a setting well suited to understanding the intricacies of a privacy claim. As a result, claims which can be highly complex and unfamiliar to judges are addressed through a hurried procedure and without lawyers to guide the case. Bringing a claim by way of class action removes, by rule, the proceeding from the purview of small claims court,[44] thereby ensuring a trial (assuming the class action is certified) and allowing claimants to benefit from legal representation.

Third, in a class proceeding class members may typically choose the degree to which they would like to participate (or not) in the litigation. As a class action is brought under the name of a representative plaintiff, claimants who wish to protect their identity are afforded a degree of separation from the suit. Class members who want a more active role in the litigation are typically able to take one on, for example by offering testimonial evidence, directing counsel, or communicating with other class members.[45] In contrast, in individual suits, claimants must bring the claim in their own name, direct counsel, and often provide evidence themselves. In administrative proceedings, the participatory rights can be restricted.

If class actions, at least theoretically, go hand in hand with all types of privacy claims, then we would expect claimants in a wide variety of privacy cases to frequently turn to class actions. A review of the jurisprudence reveals that this has not been the case.

b Practical application of class actions to privacy claims

This sub-section will review the certification and authorization motions which have been brought in Canada in privacy cases. Closer examination of these motions reveals that privacy class actions are most often brought if the case exhibits at least one of three specific factual attributes: (1) the personal information is related to the data subject's health; (2) the personal information was accessed by hacking or by a loss of a physical memory device, such as a USB (universal serial bus) key; and (3) the personal information was accessed by an employee of an organization without that organization's authorization.

Before proceeding, I must add two comments. First, I have introduced these attributes as a means to more easily discuss larger patterns in the jurisprudence. By looking broadly at characteristics of claims which are brought most frequently, my objective is to better understand practical limitations to bringing privacy class actions. These limitations will be explored in greater

---

43 See e.g. Art 542 CCP.
44 *CPA, supra* note 8 at s 1, see definition of "court."
45 Winkler et al, *supra* note 4 at 194.

detail in the following section. Second, I am not claiming that every privacy class action will contain one of these attributes. Nor are these attributes mutually exclusive; as we will see, there are cases in which personal health information (the first category) was improperly accessed by the employee of the organization holding that information (the third category).

i Personal health information

Class actions frequently arise where a large institution such as a hospital is alleged to be responsible for a privacy violation relating to personal health information. These class actions stand out for the particularly sensitive nature of personal health information, the power imbalance between hospitals and patients, and the presence of special statutory regimes to regulate personal health information in provinces such as Ontario and British Columbia.

Health-sector class actions often overlap with loss of memory device and unauthorized employee access cases. For example, in *Rowlands v Durham Region Health*,[46] a nurse lost a USB key containing the unencrypted personal information of approximately 85,000 individuals who had received an H1N1 immunization shot. Justice Lauwers certified the action, which advanced claims of negligence, a breach of fiduciary duty, and a statutory duty under the Personal Health Information Protection Act (PHIPA).[47]

In *Hopkins v Kay*,[48] the Ontario Court of Appeal upheld certification of a class proceeding relating to improper access of patient records by a nurse. The representative plaintiff, who had attended the hospital numerous times for treatment of injuries afflicted by her ex-husband, "feared that her ex-husband paid someone to access her patient records in order to find her."[49] The plaintiff claimed that the hospital had breached its statutory duties under PHIPA and had committed the tort of intrusion upon seclusion.

ii Hacking or loss of physical memory device

Following *Rowlands*, class actions were more frequently brought in instances where a physical memory device containing personal information was lost, or where electronically stored personal information was kept unsafely and accessed by hackers. For instance, in *Condon v Canada*,[50]

---

46 *Rowlands v Durham Region Health, et al*, 2011 ONSC 719 [*Rowlands*].
47 *Ibid* at para 6; *Personal Health Information Protection Act, 2004*, SO 2004, c 3, Sch A [*PHIPA*].
48 *Hopkins v Kay*, 2015 ONCA 112 [*Hopkins*].
49 *Ibid* at para 6.
50 *Condon v Canada*, 2015 FCA 159 [*Condon*].

the Federal Court of Appeal certified a class action relating to a lost hard drive at the offices of Human Resources and Skills Development Canada that contained personal information about individuals who had received student loans through the federal government program. The case is notable for being the first class action certified which included a claim of intrusion upon seclusion.

Cases where personal information is accessed through hacking have also been certified. In *Tucci v Peoples Trust Company*,[51] a financial services company did not secure its online application page, allowing unauthorized persons to access the personal information of its clients. Citing *Rowlands* extensively, the British Columbia Supreme Court certified a class action under claims of breach of contract, breach of confidence, and negligence.[52] Class actions have also been filed for the well-publicized hacking incidents related to Target[53] and Equifax.[54]

Not all such certification or authorization motions are successful. In *Sofio v Investment Industry Regulatory Organization of Canada*,[55] an IIROC employee lost a laptop containing the unencrypted personal financial information of approximately 50,000 Canadians. The claim was brought under Québec's general civil liability provision. As there was no evidence that the information had been used maliciously, the court noted that the only damages available were "of the nature of ordinary annoyances and anxieties and do not constitute 'compensable' damages."[56]

iii Unauthorized employee access

The final commonly seen scenario concerns employees impermissibly accessing personal information kept by their employer, as in *Hopkins*. Class actions have been certified where employees improperly accessed personal information related to insurance,[57] disseminated banking information for fraudulent purposes,[58] or viewed hospital records.[59] In these cases, the

51 *Tucci v Peoples Trust Company*, 2017 BCSC 1525 [*Tucci*].
52 *Ibid* at paras 195–202.
53 *Zuckerman v Target Corporation*, 2017 QCCS 110.
54 *Li c Equifax Inc*, 2018 QCCS 1892.
55 *Sofio c Organisme canadien de réglementation du commerce des valeurs mobilières (OCRCVM)*, 2015 QCCA 1820 [*Sofio*].
56 *Ibid* at para 66.
57 *Ari v Insurance Corporation of British Columbia*, 2015 BCCA 468.
58 *Evans v The Bank of Nova Scotia*, 2014 ONSC 2135.
59 *Hynes v Western Regional Integrated Health Authority*, 2014 NLTD(G) 137; *Daniells v McLellan*, 2017 ONSC 3466 [*Daniells*].

employer is always listed as a defendant, whereas the employee is only listed as a co-defendant in certain cases.

c Concluding thoughts on this section

Up to this point, I have examined the advantages offered by class actions over conventional civil proceedings. I then mapped these advantages onto some of the shortcomings inherent to bringing a privacy claim and concluded that, in theory, the advantages of class actions respond well to the difficulties associated with bringing *any* privacy claim, not just a particular subset. But this hypothesis has not been substantiated. A review of the jurisprudence shows a general pattern of privacy class actions being brought most frequently where personal health information is at stake, the information was lost or accessed by hacking, or it was accessed by an unauthorized employee. In general, the presence of specific statutory mechanisms, or cases with facts that are highly similar to a recent successful privacy tort claim, are most likely to be brought. However, outside of these instances, class actions have not fulfilled their promise to improve access to justice across all types of privacy cases.

These attributes are instructive about how privacy class actions work in practice. For example, other types of claims are brought less frequently, such as claims related to the collection of personal information without consent, unauthorized sale of personal information to data aggregators, or defamatory or other reputational harms related to the use of personal information.[60] The next section will shed light on why and how the jurisprudence has broken down along these lines.

4 Towards more widespread use of privacy class actions

Why is it that class actions are brought for some types of privacy harms more frequently than for others? This section will argue that three main factors affect privacy class actions differently depending on their factual attributes: (1) perception of the harm as "non-compensable"; (2) inherently individualized damages; and (3) business incentives of plaintiff-side class actions lawyers. Generally speaking, these factors have been less restrictive on class actions with one of the identified attributes (personal health information, hacking or loss of information, unauthorized employee access) than other types of privacy class actions.

---

60 See e.g. *Bennett v Lenovo (Canada)*, 2017 ONSC 5853 [*Bennett*].

a Cause of action: damages may not be "compensable"

Privacy class actions may be rejected by courts where the plaintiffs' injuries are easily recognizable and, more importantly, perceived as compensable by jurists. Class actions which exhibit one of the three factual attributes generally exhibit a more easily cognizable type of injury. For example, in unauthorized employee access cases, the facts are highly analogous to those in *Jones*. Following that case, the rate of privacy cases in the common law provinces increased. Similarly, when personal health information is at stake, more specific statutes provide causes of action and obligations on the holders of that information.

The cases of *Mazzonna*[61] and *Belley*[62] perfectly exemplify courts' hesitations in certifying privacy class actions because the plaintiffs did not suffer a type of injury recognized by the law. In 2008, Chrysler Financial sent a tape containing the personal information of approximately 240,000 clients from a facility in the United States to a credit agency in Rouyn Noranda, Québec, using a "regular delivery service."[63] The tape was not encrypted, did not have a backup, and was not password protected. The tape was lost. Two weeks after Chrysler was informed of the loss, it sent out a letter to the customers whose personal information was on the tape, encouraging them to "be watchful for any possible misuse of [their] personal information."[64]

Ms. Mazzonna was the representative plaintiff. She described the damages suffered by her and the class members as "anxiety, inconvenience, pain, suffering and/or fear due to the loss of their personal information."[65] Justice Lacoursière held that Chrysler had committed a fault, but emphasized that there were no allegations of identity theft or fraud. While he acknowledged that the representative plaintiff "did indeed suffer anxiety," he concluded that her "inconveniences were negligible"[66] and that her damages were "not enough to meet the threshold, however *prima facie*, of the existence of 'compensable' damages," preferring to treat them as "of the nature of ordinary annoyances."[67] Justice Lacoursière therefore held that Ms. Mazzonna had not met the first authorization criterion.

Just two months after the *Mazzonna* motion was decided, Mr. Belley filed a second motion for authorization based on the same incident.

61 *Mazzonna v DaimlerChrysler Financial Services Canada Inc*, 2012 QCCS 958 [*Mazzonna*].
62 *Belley v TD Auto Finance Services Inc*, 2015 QCCS 168 [*Belley*].
63 *Mazzonna, supra* note 61 at para 7.
64 *Ibid* at para 5.
65 *Ibid* at para 10.
66 *Ibid* at para 57.
67 *Ibid* at para 58.

Unsurprisingly, the main difference between his motion and Ms. Mazzonna's was the allegation that Mr. Belley had been the victim of identity theft and fraud. Once again, the motion was argued before Justice Lacoursière. This time, he refused to conclude that the representative plaintiff had not suffered compensable damages, noting that he could not "from a cursory look at comments on a list of potential members, conclude that the members of the Group have not suffered damages as a consequence of the Data Tape Loss."[68]

Justice Lacoursière's findings are instructive. Class actions are better suited to claims derived from more specific causes of action, such as torts already recognized at common law or statutory causes of action, rather than more general claims relying on moral or emotional injury. This conclusion is supported by empirical data. The most common types of class actions that are brought before the courts are for claims related to drugs or medical devices, price fixing, product liability, or securities misconduct.[69] Each of these areas has specific statutes and well-developed bodies of substantive law, which can be drawn upon in private law claims. In contrast, environmental or personal injury/mass tort claims are brought infrequently, partly due to difficulties in demonstrating individual damages which are "compensable."[70] As such, class actions for claims relating to privacy issues like discriminatory algorithms, whose injury may not always be "compensable" and do not arise out of a specific cause of action, will be stunted.

b Commonality: privacy's inherent individuality?

Commonality lies at the core of class actions law. Indeed, we like class actions where the plaintiffs are nearly indistinguishable from each other in relation to the defendant. This can present an obstacle for privacy claims, as, at first glance, privacy claims seem inherently individualized. For instance, for Warren and Brandeis, the privacy tort "secured people's ability to limit access to themselves and to determine the amount of personal information revealed to others and, in this way, to develop their personalities without interference."[71] However, Warren and Brandeis's classical vision is highly individualized and focuses on specific facts about a person.[72] Today, this notion is supplemented by a more collective notion which responds to

---

68 *Belley, supra* note 62 at para 66.
69 Jasminka Kalajdzic, *Class Actions in Canada: The Promise and Reality of Access to Justice* (Vancouver: UBC Press, 2017) at 16–17.
70 *Ibid.*
71 Danielle Keats Citron, "Mainstreaming Privacy Torts" (2010) 98 Cal L Rev 1805 at 1819.
72 Warren & Brandeis, *supra* note 1.

concerns created by large data repositories and data processing algorithms, which can make highly accurate guesses with thousands of data points, even if these data points are de-personalized.[73]

For class action cases exhibiting one of the three aforementioned attributes (health information, memory device loss, or unauthorized employee access), the plaintiffs are situated relatively similarly to each other, thereby more easily fulfilling the commonality requirement. Hacking or loss of device cases involve a single incident in which, presumably, the same personal information about each putative plaintiff was lost. In the case of unauthorized employee access, there is only a single individual who took the same action with respect to each of the class members. In both cases, the defendant's conduct was identical or nearly identical vis-à-vis each plaintiff, and the harm suffered can be analysed more easily on a class-wide basis.

Courts are weary of the individuality associated with privacy. Moreover, as privacy harms are frequently characterized as being essentially moral or emotional damages, they take on a highly subjective character. Consider *Ladas v Apple Inc*,[74] a case brought by users of certain iPhone, iPad, and iPod models against Apple for allegedly designing and producing devices to record and store the users' locational data without the users' consent. The Supreme Court of British Columbia held that the question of whether Apple had breached the class members' rights under the province's Privacy Act was not a common issue.[75] Justice Adair stated that its resolution "requires the court to look not only at Apple, but also at the individual circumstances of the plaintiff and other proposed class members,"[76] further noting that "it is plain that whether there has been a violation of the privacy of another must be decided on the particular facts of each case."[77]

Further complications may arise in cases where a user agreement or terms of use of an online service purport to defeat the class members' claims. Generally, the quality of the contractual consent given when entering into the agreement is in question. In Canada, in *Douez v Facebook*,[78] a case in which Facebook allegedly used its users' photos for advertising purposes without their knowledge, this obstacle was weakened slightly. Although the issue relating to consent was certified as a common issue, the court ominously noted that "depending on the evidence at trial, it is possible that

---

73 See e.g. Cofone & Robertson, *supra* note 33; Daniel J Solove & Danielle Keats Citron, "Risk and Anxiety: A Theory of Data-Breach Harms" (2018) 96 Texas L Rev 737.

74 *Ladas v Apple Inc*, 2014 BCSC 1821 [*Ladas*].

75 *Privacy Act*, RSBC 1996, c 373 [BC Privacy Act].

76 Ladas, *supra* note 74 at para 180.

77 *Ibid* at para 181.

78 *Douez v Facebook*, 2018 BCCA 186 [*Douez*].

this proceeding might devolve into individual inquiries into the issue of consent."[79] The United States has taken a different approach on this issue. In 2011, the Supreme Court of the United States enforced an arbitration clause, requiring users to arbitrate their claims individually, thereby barring them from participating in a class action.[80] Some commentators have argued that this case has had a "class-action killing" effect.[81]

c Representation: business incentives of plaintiff-side class actions lawyers

Underlying these legal explanations is a hypothesis related to the business of class actions. In Canada, there are relatively few law firms which specialize in plaintiff-side class actions litigation. Unlike most lawyers, they are not paid by the hour, but rather receive a percentage of the class's settlement or award on the merits.[82] Furthermore, the class counsel typically bears the burden of paying the defendant's legal costs in the event of an adverse decision.[83] The reward for winning a class action or securing a settlement can be lucrative, but the financial consequences of a failed certification attempt or loss on the merits can be devastating. As such, plaintiff-side class actions lawyers are disincentivized from pursuing cases in which there is high uncertainty of earning any compensation for the class (and thus for themselves), or in which the potential payout is low. As Justice Perell acknowledged:

> Fair and reasonable compensation must be sufficient to provide a real economic incentive to take on a class proceeding and to do it well. . . . The above considerations test the range of counsel fees *as an incentive for Class Counsel to take on difficult cases* in the future.[84]

It should come as no surprise that a survey of plaintiff-side counsel revealed that the two most important selection criteria were the size of the case as measured by quantum of damages and the legal merit of the claim.[85]

---

79 *Ibid* at para 84.
80 *AT&T Mobility LLC v Concepcion*, 131 S Ct 1740, 563 US 333 (2011).
81 Hubley, *supra* note 41 at 765.
82 See e.g. *Chu v Parwell Investments Inc et al*, 2019 ONSC 700.
83 Winkler et al, *supra* note 4 at 194.
84 *Fantl v Transamerica Life Canada*, [2009] OJ No. 4324 at paras 82, 98, 2009 CanLII 55704 (ONSC).
85 Kalajdzic, *supra* note 69 at 20–21.

The risk associated with bringing a privacy claim as a class action may deter plaintiff-side lawyers from taking on the case. In contrast, privacy harms which are shown to result in compensation, such as *Jones* evidencing the viability of unauthorized employee access cases, are more attractive to plaintiff-side counsel. From a business perspective, it is unwise to invest significant time and money in cases whose outcomes are less certain and which are less likely to result in a lucrative payout. Only certain types of privacy class actions may present a good business case to plaintiff-side class actions lawyers.

d (Re)definition: more widespread accessibility of the privacy class action

This chapter has identified factors which limit the more widespread use of privacy class actions. Although solutions to this problem would likely need to address elements of both class actions law and privacy law, at the heart of the issue is the law's conception of privacy. Reconceptualizing privacy harms would help overcome some of the barriers to advancing privacy class actions.

Cofone and Robertson offer one such model, which posits that knowledge of another's personal attributes is better viewed as probabilistic, rather than deterministic. Therefore, a privacy loss has occurred where there is an "increase in [an] outsider's certainty."[86] Essentially, this is when an outsider is more likely to correctly guess aspects of your personal information than they were prior to some act or event.[87] They distinguish between torts which protect "true privacy interests," such as intrusion upon seclusion and public disclosure of private facts, and torts which protect "reputational interests," such as defamation. Similarly, Solove and Citron argue that in cases of data breaches, U.S. courts are overly dismissive of privacy harms, such as the increased risk of identity theft and fraud, or anxiety. They draw upon existing jurisprudence to demonstrate how judges could assess risk and anxiety.[88]

Applying these models more widely to privacy torts and possibly statutory causes of action would facilitate privacy class action certification. Claimants would more easily be able to demonstrate a cause of action, as privacy injuries would be "compensable"; commonality among the plaintiffs would be increased, as the subjectivity that is associated with viewing a

---

86 Cofone & Robertson, *supra* note 33 at 1049. See also Ignacio N Cofone (2020 forthcoming) "Harm in Privacy Class Actions" (on file with author).

87 *Ibid.*

88 Solove & Citron, *supra* note 73.

privacy harm as emotional injury or an annoyance would be mitigated; and a greater likelihood of certification would also reduce the risk for plaintiff-side counsel to take on privacy cases.

Regardless of the path forward, the core issue is the inaccessibility of privacy class actions. Any path forward will need to consider deeply rooted conceptions of privacy in the law and in society.

5 Conclusion

I have reviewed privacy class actions in Canada, demonstrating that they arise most frequently where personal health information was at stake, where the information was accessed by a hacker or by accidental loss, or where an employee accessed personal information held by their employer in an unauthorized manner. Each of these cases situates the plaintiffs similarly to the defendant and more easily allows jurists to be cognizant of the harm suffered and the causes of action. As such, the financial risk associated with representing a class is mitigated, making potential counsel more likely to take on these types of privacy cases.

More widespread use of privacy class actions is facing serious barriers. In particular, privacy harms are frequently dismissed as giving rise to damages which are "non-compensable" and tend to be characterized as subjective, individualized harms, making it difficult to litigate these cases on a common basis. Reconceptualizing privacy harms would make privacy class actions, and therefore enforcement of privacy rights, more effective. I have suggested Cofone and Robertson's statistical model of privacy harms and Solove and Citron's analysis of risk and anxiety as promising possibilities.

As both privacy cases and class actions continue to garner greater attention from jurists, a richer body of doctrine and jurisprudence will develop. Substantial changes to both privacy and class actions law must take place before class actions fulfil their promises of access to justice, judicial economy, and behaviour modification for privacy claims.

3 Uncertainties and lessons learned from data protection laws

Eloïse Gratton and Lauren Phizicky

1 Introduction

Privacy class action lawsuits are a growing trend in Canada, with over 80 cases across the country in recent years. In terms of monetary damages for privacy violations, these privacy class actions pose a significant threat for Canadian businesses, given that private-sector privacy regulators have limited powers to issue any type of fines or penalties, unlike their European counterparts.[1]

More than half of these class action cases have been filed in Ontario. In 2012, the Court of Appeal for Ontario recognized a new tort of "intrusion upon seclusion" for the first time in Canada in *Jones v. Tsige*.[2] This new tort has made privacy class actions potentially viable because it appears to allow victims to advance compensation claims for privacy breaches without proof of economic harm and without regard for the victim's individual circumstances. A large number of these claims have been filed in Quebec, where an "invasion of privacy" civil tort exists under the Civil Code of Quebec,[3] as

---

1 The Federal Privacy Commissioner and privacy regulators in Alberta and British Columbia can issue fines of up to $10,000 in the case of an individual and $100,000 in the case of an organization for certain specific violations of their respective acts, and the privacy regulator in Quebec can issue fines of up to $50,000 for a first offence (although to date it has never exercised this power), whereas fines under the GDPR can be up to €20 million, or 4% of annual global turnover in the case of an organization – whichever is higher. *Personal Information Protection Act*, SA 2003, c P-6.5, s 59(2) [*Alberta PIPA*]; *Personal Information Protection Act*, SBC 2003, c 63, s56(2) [*BC PIPA*]; *Act Respecting the Protection of Personal Information in the Private Sector*, CQLR c P-39.1, s 91 [*Personal Information Private Sector Act*]; *Personal Information Protection and Electronic Documents Act*, SC 2000, c 5, s 28 [*PIPEDA*]; EC, *Regulation (EU) 2016/679* of 27 April 2016 on the protection of natural persons with regard to the processing of personal data and on the free movement of such data, and repealing Directive 95/46/EC (General Data Protection Regulation), [2016] OJ, L 119, art 83 [*GDPR*].
2 *Jones v Tsige*, 2012 ONCA 32 [*Jones*].
3 Art 35–36 CCQ.

well as under the Quebec Charter of Human Rights and Freedoms,[4] which applies to private-sector organizations. Privacy statutes in other provinces, such as those in British Columbia, Newfoundland and Labrador, Saskatchewan and Manitoba,[5] can also be the legal basis of these claims.

While some of these privacy class action lawsuits have settled for large amounts[6] – possibly to avoid expensive and lengthy trials, reputational impact and disclosure obligations – none of them have proceeded to trial or been heard on their merits.

Privacy class actions typically fall into one of two categories: actions related to the failure to protect personal information using adequate security measures, and those relating to the launch of a potentially intrusive business model. More than half of privacy class action cases make up the first category and deal with "security breaches", either as the result of a cyber-attack,[7]

---

4 *Charter of Human Rights and Freedoms*, CQL c C-12.

5 BC: *Privacy Act*, RSBC 1996, c 373; Sask: *Privacy Act*, RSS 1978, c P-24; Man: *Privacy Act*, RSM 1987 c P-125; NL: *Privacy Act*, RSN 1990, c P-22. The Court did not refer to Alberta.

6 See e.g. Barry Glaspell, "The Increasing Settlement Costs of Mass Privacy Breaches" (2018) 13:2 Canadian Class Action Rev 335.

7 See e.g. *Maksimovic v Sony*, 2013 ONSC 4604 [*Maksimovic*]; *Lozanski v Home Depot, Inc*, 2016 ONSC 5447 [*Lozanski*]; *Karasik v. Yahoo! Inc et al* (ONT)[*Karasik*]; *Demers c Yahoo! Inc*, 2017 QCCS 4154 [*Demers*]; *Gill v Yahoo! Canada Co, et al*, 2018 BCSC 290 [*Gill*]; *Banadyga v Wal-Mart Canada Corp*, 2016 SKQB 405 [*Banadyga*]; *Drew v Walmart Canada Inc*, 2016 ONSC 8067 [*Drew 2016*]; *Drew v Walmart Canada Inc*, 2017 ONSC 3308 [*Drew 2017*]; *Zuckerman v Target Corp*, 2015 QCCS 1285 [*Zuckerman 2015*]; *Sofio c Organisme canadien de réglementation du commerce des valeurs mobilières (OCRCVM)*, 2015 QCCA 1820 [*Sofio*]; *Zuckerman v Target Corporation*, 2017 QCCS 110 [*Zuckerman 2017*]; *Tucci v Peoples Trust*, 2013 [*Tucci 2013*]; *Tucci v Peoples Trust Company*, 2015 BCSC 987 [*Tucci 2015*]; *Tucci v Peoples Trust Company*, 2017 BCSC 1525 [*Tucci 2017*]; *Kaplan v Casino Rama Services Inc*, 2017 ONSC 2671 [*Kaplan*]; *Azam v Inc and Equifax Canada Co*, Notice of Civil Claim, filed on September 18, 2017 [*Azam*]; *Ballantine v Equifax* [*Ballantine*]; *Agnew-Americano v Equifax Canada*, 2018 ONSC 275 [*Agnew-Americano*]; in BC and SK: *Joshua Elliott Temple v Equifax Inc and EquifaX Canada Co*, VLC-S-S-180347 [*Joshua*]; *Daniel Thalheimer v Equifax* [*Thalheimer*]; In QC: *Li c Equifax Inc*, 200-06-000885-174 [*Li*]; in ONT: *Laura Ballantine and Equifax Inc, and Equifax Canada Co*, File No CV-17-582566 [*Ballantine v Equifax*]; *Setoguchi v Uber* [*Setoguchi*]; *Fortier c Uber Canada Inc, Uber Technologies Inc, Uber B.V et Rasier Operations B.V*, QSC, No: 500-06-000902-185, January 23, 2018 [*Fortier*]; *Steinman v CIBC*, ONSC, CV-18-00599875-00, June 15, 2018 [*Steinman*]; *Wilson v Bank of Montreal*, ONSC, CV-18-00599876-00, June 15, 2018 [*Wilson*]; *Levy v Nissan Canada Inc*, QSC, 500-06-000907-184, February 12, 2018 [*Levy*]; *Marriott International Inc, Marriott Hotels of Canada Ltd and Starwood Canada ULC* [*Marriott*]; in NS: *Mann v Marriott* [*Mann*]; BC: *Krygier v Marriott* [*Krygier*]; *Wong v Marriott* [*Wong*], *James v Marriott* [*James*]; in ONT: *Schnarr and Brown* [*Schnarr & Brown*]; in BC: *Sache v Marriott* [*Sache*]; in QC: *Won Kil Bai v Marriott* [*Won Kil Bai*]; in AB: *Loveseth v Marriott* [*Loveseth*].

loss of device, other types of theft of personal information[8] or unauthorized access – for instance, a number of cases involve employee "snooping" on personal information that they should not have accessed.[9]

The second category of class actions, which relates to the launch of a potentially intrusive business model, comprises about 20 of the privacy class action cases in Canada. In those cases, an organization either conducted illegal business practices involving personal information or failed to adequately inform and/or obtain proper consent for a business practice.[10]

The activities that lead to these two types of class actions (security incidents and intrusive business models) involve the management of personal information. These activities (i.e. protecting personal information using adequate security measures or obtaining proper consent before collecting, using or disclosing personal information) include business practices that are usually regulated by data protection laws.

In this chapter, we suggest that it can be a challenge to rely on privacy torts to understand and qualify the types of wrongdoing or causes of action relevant to these privacy class action cases and to quantify the related damages that could be claimed. These privacy tort laws do not specifically regulate the collection, use, disclosure and protection of personal information. They generally prohibit activities such as surveillance, eavesdropping, spying, listening to or recording of conversations; the unauthorized use of the name or likeness or voice of a person; or the use of personal letters, diaries and other personal documents without the individual's prior consent, rather than the management of personal information. We also articulate the view

---

8 See e.g. *Lamoureux v Investment Industry Regulatory Organization of Canada (IIROC)*, 2016 QCCS 4704 [*Lamoureux*]; *Condon v Canada*, 2014 FC 250 [*Condon 2014*]; *Condon v Canada*, 2015 FCA 159 [*Condon 2015*]; *Condon v Canada*, 2018 FC 522 [*Condon 2018*].

9 See e.g. *Mallinson v Trillium Health Partners, Dr. A. Tony Vettese and Lisa Lyons* [*Mallinson*]; *Daniells v McLellan*, 2017 ONSC 3466 [*Daniells*]; and *Murray v East Coast Forensic Hospital*, 2015 NSSC 61 [*Murray 2015*]; *Capital District Health Authority v Murray*, 2017 NSCA 28 [*Murray 2017*].

10 These cases have been filed against large technology companies such as Apple, Facebook, Google and Bell. See e.g. *Union des Consommateurs c Bell*, 2011 QCCS 1118 [*Union des Consommateurs*]; *Plimmer v Google Inc*, 2013 BCSC 681 [*Plimmer*]; *Albilia v Apple Inc*, 2013 QCCS 2805 [*Albilia 2013*]; *Albilia v Apple Inc*, 2014 QCCS 5311 [*Albilia 2014*]; *Ladas v Apple Inc*, 2014 BCSC 1821 [*Ladas*]; *Chasles v Bell Canada inc*, 2017 QCCS 5200 [*Chasles*]; *Austin v Bell Canada*, 2018 ONSC 4018 [*Austin*]; *Emond and MacQueen v Google LLC*, CV-18-590521, 2018 [*Emond & MacQueen*]; *Lima v Google LLC*, QSC, No: 500-06-000940-183 and 500-06-000940-185, August 15, 2018 [*Lima*]; *Leventakis v Facebook, Inc*, QSC, No: 500-06-000938-189, July 20, 2018 [*Leventakis*]; *Elkoby v Google inc/ Google*, 2018 QCCS 2623 [*Elkoby*]; *Stuart Thiel and Brianna Thicke c Facebook* Inc and Facebook Canada Ltd [*Thiel&Thicke*]; *Chamberlain v Facebook, Inc and Facebook Canada Inc*, ONT, CV-18-598747OOCP [*Chamberlain*].

that by turning to the types of obligations that data protection laws set out for organizations for managing personal information and the type of damages that might be claimed following a breach of an organization's data protection obligations, it becomes apparent that fault cannot always be clearly established and claims of damages can be challenged.

2 Privacy wrongdoing

In Canada, the federal Personal Information Protection and Electronic Documents Act (PIPEDA) sets out ground rules for how private-sector organizations collect, use and disclose personal information about individuals,[11] unless such activities are regulated by provincial legislation that has been declared substantially similar to PIPEDA. The provinces of British Columbia,[12] Alberta[13] and Quebec[14] have enacted provincial data protection legislation that is recognized as substantially similar to PIPEDA,[15] and therefore in those provinces, this legislation operates in place of PIPEDA for intra-provincial matters.[16] Failure to comply with PIPEDA or the provincial laws from British Columbia, Alberta and Quebec ("Data Protection Laws") can result in regulatory investigations and published findings (decisions) from the federal Privacy Commissioner of Canada (OPC) or regulatory investigations and orders from the provincial regulators.

One of the issues is that by attempting to draft Data Protection Laws that are flexible and technology neutral, the result has been laws that can seem vague. The Data Protection Laws are based on old privacy principles, imported from Europe, that date back to the late 1960s and early 1970s and also formed the basis of the Organisation for Economic Co-operation and Development (OECD) Guidelines.[17] At that time, with the development of

---

11 *PIPEDA, supra* note 3, s 3. PIPEDA is applicable to organizations carrying on "federal work, undertaking or business" (s 2 "federal work, undertaking or business"; s 4(1)(b)) and organizations in provinces and territories where no personal information protection act has been enacted, such as Ontario (i.e. all provinces except Quebec, Alberta and British Columbia).

12 *BC PIPA, supra* note 3.

13 *Alberta PIPA, supra* note 3.

14 *An Act respecting the Protection of Personal Information in the Private Sector*, RSQ, c. P-39.1 (*Personal Information Private Sector Act, supra* note 3) [*Quebec ARPPIPS*].

15 *PIPEDA, supra* note 3 at subparagraph 26(2)(b).

16 *PIPEDA* also applies to federal works, undertakings and businesses, such as banks and telecommunication companies, even for intra-provincial matters in a province where a substantially similar law has been enacted.

17 Eloïse Gratton, *Understanding Personal Information: Managing Privacy Risks* (Montreal: LexisNexis Canada, 2013) at 7–11.

automated data banks and the growing use of computers in the private and public sector, privacy was conceived of as individuals being "in control over their personal information".[18] The principles of Fair Information Practices (FIPs) were elaborated during this period and have since been incorporated in Data Protection Laws adopted in various jurisdictions around the world.[19] Under these FIPs, individuals have certain rights, including the right to be informed of what personal information is collected about them, the use and the disclosure that will be made of their information and the right to consent to such data handling activities. Organizations must also protect personal information using adequate security measures.

In Canada, the FIPs were incorporated into PIPEDA and the provincial laws that have been deemed substantially similar to PIPEDA and form the basis of these laws.[20] For example, PIPEDA was drafted on the basis of flexible principles (or "soft law") intended to be technology neutral so that it would be easier for it to apply to new types of technologies.[21] Given this flexible construction, it is understandably difficult for organizations to discern what practices will be considered compliant with PIPEDA, and it is equally difficult for privacy regulators to take a single position on each issue that can remain unchanged over time.[22] This flexibility explains in part why PIPEDA establishes an ombudsman model for overseeing compliance.

18 Alan F Westin, *Privacy and Freedom* (New York: Atheneum Press, 1967).
19 See Eloïse Gratton, "Section 1.1 The Historical Background Leading to Laws Protection Personal Information" in *Understanding Personal Information: Managing Privacy Risks* (Montreal: LexisNexis Canada, 2013).
20 E.g. the fundamental principles of PIPEDA are found in its Schedule 1, which is based on the Canadian Standards Association's Model Code for the Protection of Personal Information, which, in turn, incorporates the FIPs. Organizations subject to PIPEDA must comply with the obligations set out in Schedule 1, as modified in some cases in specific provisions contained within the body of the statute itself. The FIPs are also the principles of the OECD's Guidelines on the Protection of Privacy and Transborder Flows of Personal Data (1980).
21 See Innovation, Science and Economic Development Canada, *Strengthening Privacy for the Digital Age, Proposals to Modernize the Personal Information Protection and Electronic Documents Act*, May 2019: "It should also be recognized, though, that non-compliance can sometimes be the result of a lack of clarity or certainty in terms of organizations' obligations under the Act. Organizations may want to comply but have difficulty understanding what they need to do in certain circumstances." And "Although praised for being principles based and technology neutral, PIPEDA has been criticized for being difficult to understand" referring to Dr. Teresa Scassa, who has summarized these criticisms in her blog, Teresa Scassa, "PIPEDA Reform Should Include a Comprehensive Rewrite" (July 9, 2018), online (blog): *Teresa Scassa* <www.teresascassa.ca/index.php?option=com_k2&view=item&id=279:pipeda-reform-should-include-a-comprehensive-rewrite&Itemid=80>.
22 Ibid.

This model allows organizations to innovate without great risk, since they do not need to be concerned about potential fines if they misevaluate the social norm in place at the time or the "reasonable expectation" of consumers. Instead, organizations have the opportunity to interact with the OPC and adjust their activities before they are faced with fines or other penalties, which has enabled the elaboration of PIPEDA's requirements through a gradual, bottom-up process that involves a back-and-forth between businesses and the OPC.

a Data security incidents

Under Canadian Data Protection Laws, organizations must protect personal information that they handle against loss or theft, as well as unauthorized access, disclosure, copying, use or modification.[23] They are also required to employ security safeguards that are commensurate to the sensitivity of the information involved.[24]

Whether an organization can be said to meet its safeguard obligations under the Data Protection Laws will vary depending on the facts of each complaint and investigation. Over time, findings on certain key issues have crystallized into general principles that can serve as helpful guidance for organizations. For example, if there is a security breach, privacy regulators will usually verify that the organization had the proper policies, practices and procedures in place. For instance, case law confirms that if staff use laptops away from the workplace, the organization is expected to have a policy that specifically addresses personal information and computing equipment outside the workplace.[25] If staff use email or fax to exchange personal information, organizations must develop policies that address these practices,[26] and they are also expected to develop policies for retention and secure

---

23 These requirements are found in *PIPEDA, supra* note 3, s 4.7; *Quebec ARPPIPS, supra* note 16, s 10; *Alberta PIPA, supra* note 3, s 34 and *BC PIPA, supra* note 3, s 34.

24 Office of the Privacy Commissioner of Canada, *PIPEDA Case Summary #2001–5* (2001) [*PIPEDA Case Summary #2001–5*]; Office of the Privacy Commissioner of Canada, *PIPEDA Case Summary #2002–72* (2002) [*PIPEDA Case Summary #2002–72*]; Office of the Privacy Commissioner of Canada, *PIPEDA Case Summary #2002–177* (2002) [*PIPEDA Case Summary #2002–177*]; Office of the Privacy Commissioner of Canada, *PIPEDA Case Summary #2003–180* (2003) [*PIPEDA Case Summary #2003–180*]; Office of the Privacy Commissioner of Canada, *PIPEDA Report of Findings #2012–009* (2012) [*PIPEDA Report 2012*]; Office of the Privacy Commissioner of Canada, *PIPEDA Report of Findings #2014–003* (2014) [*PIPEDA Report 2014*].

25 Office of the Information and Privacy Commissioner of Alberta, *Implementing Reasonable Safeguards, Personal Information Protection Act. Advisory #8* [*OIPC AB Advisory 8*].

26 *Ibid.*

disposal of personal information, inclusive of all formats and media (paper, electronic, video, etc.).[27] The challenge is that it is often up to the organization to determine the type and content of policies, processes and procedures necessary and sufficient to properly address their security risks. With business practices and technology constantly evolving, they have to reassess on an ongoing basis whether these current policies and procedures remain adequate and that there are no gaps between these policy documents and the actual practices.

Following a breach, privacy regulators will usually consider the corporate culture, i.e. whether employees were properly made aware of the organization's policies and processes and whether they had received the appropriate privacy training.[28] While it is clear that organizations must make their employees aware of the importance of maintaining the confidentiality of personal information,[29] there will always be some leeway and uncertainty about whether employees were sufficiently trained. For example, in the recent Report of Findings #2019–001, the OPC found that although the organization asserted that it provided employees with appropriate data handling training, the company did not have specific training relating to the "file share" network storage area that contained the personal information of approximately 8,000 Canadians and was one of the sources of the data breach. The OPC also considered that the organization's training was otherwise inadequate after it discovered, for example, that its security training regarding payment card security was "an off-the-shelf product designed for

---

27 *Ibid.* PIPEDA Case Summary #2002–72, *supra* note 26; Office of the Privacy Commissioner of Canada, *PIPEDA Case Summary #2003–128* (2003) [*PIPEDA Case Summary #2003–128*]; Office of the Privacy Commissioner of Canada, *PIPEDA Case Summary #2006–356* (2006) [*PIPEDA Case Summary #2006–356*].

28 If the organization can demonstrate that it has the proper policies in place, it might still be held responsible if the privacy regulator finds that employees were not sufficiently informed of the relevant policies. Office of the Information and Privacy Commissioner of Alberta, *Investigation Report P2005-IR-006* (Report of an Investigation Concerning the Disclosure and Security of Personal Information, CBV Collection Services Ltd, July 21, 2005) [*AB OIPC Report 2005*]; OIPC AB Advisory 8, *supra* note 25. See *Centre Financier aux Entreprises Desjardins Grandes Seigneuries Vallée des Tisserands v Syndicat des Employées et Employés Professionnels et de Bureau*, Section Locale 575, AZ-50507770 [*Desjardins*].

29 Under *PIPEDA*, *supra* note 3 at Principle 4.7.4. See also Office of the Information and Privacy Commissioner of Alberta, *Investigation Report #P2006-IR-003* [*AB OIPC Report 2006*]: Staff of a beauty supply organization disposed of customer personal information in a dumpster. The organization did not provide adequate direction regarding the confidential and secure disposal of records, and staff only tore the records by hand instead of shredding them.

front line retail staff and supervisors" which had not been tailored to the organization.[30]

Businesses also have certain security obligations when the personal information under its control is transferred to a third party (i.e. its partners and service providers) for processing and usually must, as a security measure, enter into a signed agreement to confirm the third party's security commitments.[31] If there is a security breach, privacy regulators will usually verify that the organization had proper contracts in place with service providers who may be accessing or managing personal information.[32] While the requirement to have a contract is clear from the reading of the law, the content of such a contract was until recently left to the discretion of the organization. Again, in its Report of Findings regarding the 2017 Equifax data breach, the OPC recently provided more guidance on what it expects in terms of content and indicated that the following details should generally be included in these outsourcing agreements: what personal information is being handled by the third party; what specific rules, regulations and standards need to be complied with in the handling of the information, including applicable Data Protection Laws; the roles and responsibilities of key stakeholders within both organizations for the handling of the personal information, including responsibilities for specific functions, decision-making, safeguards and breach response; information security obligations; acceptable uses of the information; retention and destruction obligations; and reporting and oversight arrangements to ensure compliance with applicable Data Protection Laws, including reporting obligations in the case of a breach that could compromise the personal information.[33]

While the non-binding findings from the OPC on certain key issues have crystallized into general principles that can serve as helpful guidance for organizations, the position of privacy regulators may change over time as security standards evolve and other jurisdictions adopt privacy legislation. Also, privacy regulators will generally consider what the current state-of-the-art standards, such as technical standards, are in determining whether

---

30 Office of the Privacy Commissioner of Canada, *PIPEDA Report of Findings #2019–001*, Investigation into Equifax Inc. and Equifax Canada Co.'s compliance with PIPEDA in light of the 2017 breach of personal information (April 9, 2019) [*PIPEDA Report 2019*].

31 See *PIPEDA supra* note 3 at principle 4.1.3; *BC PIPA supra* note 3, s 4(2); *Alberta PIPA, supra* note 3, s 5(2); *Quebec ARPPIPS, supra* note 16, s 20.

32 Office of the Privacy Commissioner of Canada, *PIPEDA Case Summary #2007–377* (2007) [*PIPEDA Case Summary #2007–377*]. More specifically, organizations that transfer their clients' personal information to third parties must ensure that these third parties have proper safeguards in place for protecting personal information.

33 PIPEDA Report 2019, *supra* note 30 at para 74.

an organization is complying with PIPEDA. The constantly evolving nature of technology can therefore create additional challenges for an organization trying to determine what the appropriate technical standards are that should be used to protect personal information in order to comply with applicable Data Protection Laws.

For instance, in one of the earlier security breaches involving retailer TJX, the fact that drivers' license numbers and financial information were not properly encrypted was a cause of liability.[34] The OPC conducted a joint investigation with the Alberta privacy regulator, concluding that TJX had an encryption standard (Wired Equivalent Privacy [WEP]), which was outdated, and that the company was in the process of converting to a higher standard (Wi-Fi Protected Access [WPA]) at the time of the breach.[35] Authors have raised the concern that security standards evolve so quickly that by the time the privacy regulators' Report of Findings regarding TJX was published, the new encryption standard it referred to as being adequate (WPA) was already outdated.[36] More recently, in Report of Findings #2019–001, the OPC found that several of an organization's practices did not conform to internationally accepted standards for access controls. For instance, staff and customer usernames and passwords were unencrypted, production data and test data were stored in the same environment, the Secure Sockets Layer (SSL) certificate had not been renewed and the database that contained credit card information for some consumers was not included in the scope of the organization's Payment Card Industry Data Security Standard.

While privacy regulators' decisions are useful to guide organizations in making an assessment as to which security standards are adequate, given that these evolve quickly, organizations cannot limit themselves to only relying on these decisions to determine what their legal obligations are. Rather, they should also consider following guidance documents from the privacy regulators and other technical experts or survey documents to determine whether their security safeguards are up-to-date and likely to be considered to comply with the obligations under the Data Protection Laws.[37]

---

34 Office of the Privacy Commissioner of Canada, *PIPEDA Case Summary #2008–395*, Safeguards complaint against CIBC (January 2008) [*PIPEDA Case Summary #2008–395*]; Office of the Privacy Commissioner of Canada & Office of the Information and Privacy Commissioner of Alberta, *Report of an Investigation into the Security, Collection and Retention of Personal Information, PIPEDA Report of Findings #2007–389*, TJX Companies Inc. / Winners Merchant International LP (September 25, 2007) [*PIPEDA Report of Findings #2007–389*].

35 PIPEDA Report of Findings #2007–389, *supra* note 34 at para 80.

36 Nicolas Vermeys, *Responsabilité civile et sécurité informationnelle* (Montréal: Yvon Blais, 2010).

37 The annual Privacy Governance Report published annually jointly by E&Y and the International Association of Privacy Professionals can be useful at least for benchmarking, i.e.

It is important to keep in mind that the mere occurrence of a data breach does not automatically mean the organization failed to meet its safeguarding obligation under Data Protection Laws; rather, compliance will turn on whether the security safeguards in place at the time of the incident were reasonable and appropriate in the circumstances.[38] For example, it is possible, even if there is a security breach,[39] that an organization will be found not to be in violation of the applicable Data Protection Law, since the security standard acknowledges that reasonable does not mean perfect. This was the case, for instance, in *Lozanski v. The Home Depot, Inc.*, in which Home Depot was the victim of computer hacking that resulted in the credit card information of more than 56 million customers being exposed.[40] In the Superior Court's decision to approve a settlement of the class action, the Court expressed the following: "In the immediate case, given that: (a) Home Depot apparently did nothing wrong; (b) it responded in a responsible, prompt, generous, and exemplary fashion to the criminal acts perpetrated on it by the computer hackers; (c) Home Depot needed no behaviour management; (d) the Class Members' likelihood of success against Home Depot both on liability and on proof of any consequent damages was in the range of negligible to remote; and (e) the risk and expense of failure in the litigation were correspondingly substantial and proximate, I would have approved a discontinuance of Mr. Lozanski's proposed class action with or without costs and without any benefits achieved by the putative Class Members."[41]

b Intrusive business model

Under the Data Protection Laws, organizations must generally obtain an individual's meaningful consent to the collection, use or disclosure of the

---

determining what type of security standards are used by other businesses surveyed in recent months. IAPP-EY, *Annual Governance Report 2018* (2018) at 105ff [*IAPP-EY Report*], which illustrates that ISO 27001 is still the most common certification required of vendors.

38 Vermeys articulates the view that on the issue of their obligation to protect personal information using adequate measures, organizations would have a very strong obligation of diligence, but not one of guarantee. See Vermeys, *supra* note 36. See also Office of the Information and Privacy Commissioner for British Columbia, *Investigation Report F06–01, Sale of Provincial Government Computer Tapes Containing Personal Information* (March 31, 2006) [*OIPC BC Report F06–01*].

39 OIPC AB Advisory 8, *supra* note 25: "(. . .) Personal information security breaches may still occur, even where reasonable safeguards have been implemented. Instead, the reasonableness standard requires organizations to take into account all relevant circumstances in determining what safeguards to implement."

40 *Lozanski*, *supra* note 7.

41 *Ibid* at para 70.

individual's personal information.[42] The appropriate form of consent (i.e. express or opt-in, implied or opt-out) is flexible and will vary depending on the circumstances. Under PIPEDA, the form of consent should be determined in light of the sensitivity of the information and the "individual's reasonable expectations".[43] On the issue of sensitivity of the data, PIPEDA does not include a list of special categories of sensitive data, unlike the GDPR.[44] Instead, PIPEDA provides that "any information can be sensitive, depending on the context".[45] It is therefore sometimes a challenge for an organization to determine what type of information should be considered sensitive information.[46] Will it be considered that a provider of on-demand Internet streaming media that is delivering targeted advertising is using *sensitive information*? Potentially, if we consider that certain categories of shows may be more sensitive than others – for instance shows promoting violent, horror or adult content, or disclosing the personal interests of the individual, such as sexual orientation or religion, etc.

This issue of "individual's reasonable expectations" can also be difficult to assess. For example, after a Canadian telecommunications company launched a relevant advertising program a few years back, the OPC investigated the practice and concluded that the type of consent obtained should have been opt-in instead of opt-out.[47] In its Report of Findings, the OPC articulated the view that:

> 'Reasonable expectations' is an objective standard which requires that our Office consider *all of the relevant contextual* factors surrounding the practice in question, including the type of services the organization offers, and the nature of the relationship between the organization and its customers. *These contextual factors must not be considered in isolation but rather, evaluated as a whole* (emphasis added).[48]

---

42 *PIPEDA, supra* note 3, clause 4.3.

43 *PIPEDA, supra* note 3, s 6.1 which further specifies that the consent of an individual is only valid if it is reasonable to expect that an individual to whom the organization's activities are directed would understand the nature, purpose and consequences of the collection; use; or disclosure of personal information to which they are consenting.

44 *GDPR, supra* note 3.

45 *PIPEDA, supra* note 3, s 4.3.4.

46 Eloïse Gratton, "What Is Sensitive Information?" (October 24, 2014), online (blog): *Eloïse Gratton* <www.eloisegratton.com/blog/2014/10/24/what-is-sensitive-information/?repeat=w3tc>.

47 In the "Results of its Investigation into Bell Canada" section in PIPEDA Report of Findings #2015–001. See Office of the Privacy Commissioner of Canada, *PIPEDA Report of Findings #2015–001* (2015) [*PIPEDA Report of Findings #2015–001*].

48 *Ibid.*

The OPC in this decision determined that customers would reasonably expect their telecommunications provider to obtain opt-in consent *in light of all the contextual factors* surrounding the relevant advertising program.[49] It is yet to be determined if a similar decision would have been reached by the OPC on the consent issue if the organization was, for example, promoting its own products instead of enabling the delivery of third-party advertising. Decisions like this, which demonstrate how fact-specific the determination of "reasonable expectations" can be, show how it can be very difficult for companies to be confident that their innovative business models will comply with Data Protection Laws.

The notion of "reasonable expectations" is also included in a more general reasonableness test under PIPEDA: an organization may collect, use or disclose personal information only for purposes that a reasonable person would consider appropriate in the circumstances.[50] What these reasonable expectations are in any given context, and whether certain activities are legitimate from a privacy perspective, is often a function of many factors, including the social norms that are in place at the relevant period of time that may affect the users' expectations regarding such new technology or business practices.

Social norms are constantly evolving, and individuals may even sometimes change their mind about whether a technology violates their privacy. For instance, it is reported that when caller ID was launched in the late 1980s, many people considered it to be a privacy violation to see who was calling a person, to the point where some U.S. states regulated against it.[51] Today, many users refuse to answer the phone if the calling number is not displayed on their caller ID, and therefore this technology is now considered a privacy-enhancing technology.[52]

---

49 These factors in this case were that the telco: (i) began using information it already collected for the purposes of delivering its primary services for the new secondary purpose of delivering behaviorally targeted ads; (ii) delivered paid services, for which customers may pay up to hundreds of dollars per month; (iii) was enabling the delivery of third-party ads; and (iv) was a telecommunications service provider to whom users must entrust vast amounts of their sensitive personal information in order to gain access to mobile, internet, telephone and television communications in Canada.

50 *PIPEDA, supra* note 3, Sch 1, s 5(3). In Europe, legitimate interests are relevant when assessing lawful processing: see Article 29 Data Protection Working Party, *Opinion 06/2014 on the Notion of Legitimate Interests of the Data Controller under Article 7 of Directive 95/46/EC*, 844/14/EN WP 217 [*Opinion 06/2014*].

51 Steven Oates, "Caller ID: Privacy Protector or Privacy Invader" (1992) U Ill L Rev 219.

52 Omer Tene & Jules Polonetsky, "A Theory of Creepy: Technology, Privacy and Shifting Social Norms" (2013) 16 Yale JL & Tech 59 at 11.

The law and social norms will always lag behind technology. A good example of this involves cameras and the evolving social norms around them. In 1890, Samuel Warren and Louis Brandeis first formulated the concept of the modern legal right to privacy in their famous article about the "right to be let alone", which they wrote in reaction to the threat of "instantaneous photography" in the popular press that was then invading the sacred precincts of private and domestic life.[53] Still, it took another 70 years for the United States to elaborate relevant common law privacy torts.[54] More recently, the ubiquity of cameras on mobile phones has created a new distortion, and the social norm surrounding cameras is, once again, not quite in place. While walking around a gym's locker room with a digital camera in hand would probably be considered to violate a social norm and be inappropriate, many still continue to carry around their camera-enabled phones in locker rooms, perhaps given that this dual functionality is still relatively recent. The evolution of this norm has led certain gyms to post signs warning that cellphone cameras should not be used in locker rooms.[55]

In some situations, a corporation's deployment of a new technology or some new use of an existing technology, the implementation of a new feature or program or an unexpected data use or customization may be seen as going against social norms regarding privacy.[56] However, this makes for a difficult landscape for innovative corporations to operate within, since these innovations may not necessarily rise to the level of breaching any laws, including the Data Protection Laws. This uncertainty is increased by the fact that the reasonableness test now incorporates a contextual approach for determining which type of consent is adequate in a given scenario (which applies notwithstanding the fact that consent was obtained).

Although this uncertainty makes it difficult for organizations seeking to launch an innovative product or service to know exactly where to draw the line on whether their practices are reasonable ones, this uncertainty is also part of the reason why PIPEDA still operates under an ombudsman model, as discussed above. When assessing the class actions against some of the large technology companies related to intrusive business practices, we must keep in mind the flexibility inherent in PIPEDA's construction

---

53 Samuel D Warren & Louis D Brandeis, "The Right to Privacy" (1890) 4:5 Harv L Rev 193. It led the *New York Times* in 1902 to decry "Kodakers lying in wait".

54 William L Prosser, "Privacy" (1960) 48 Cal L Rev 383; see also *Restatement (Second) of Torts* § 652D (1976).

55 Catherine Saint Louis, "Cellphones Test Strength of Gym Rules", *New York Times* (December 7, 2011).

56 Tene & Polonetsky, *supra* note 53 at 2.

and the ombudsman model that is meant to allow companies to consult with the OPC before incurring real consequences. The notion of whether certain practices were legal and whether an organization is at fault should be assessed with the same flexibility as the determination of whether the practice was compliant with Data Protection Laws.

3 Damages

The type of damage, and thus the level of damages, can be very different from one breach situation to the next. For instance, the type of damage triggered for consumers after a transaction database or a database of credentials is hacked, which can trigger a risk of fraud or identity theft, is very different from the type of damage triggered following a situation like the Ashley Madison incident, where the users of the online dating site for people already in relationships were revealed online after the site was hacked. In the latter situation, the harm triggered was of a risk of humiliation and reputational damage, among other things. The ultimate purpose of Data Protection Laws is to protect individuals from the *risk of harm* – rather than only the actual harm – that may result from the collection, use or disclosure of their information.[57] While the collection or disclosure of personal information may trigger a more subjective kind of harm, the use of information – such as to commit fraud against that person – may trigger a more objective kind of harm.[58] While this distinction may be useful to determine the type of harm that could come into play in some of these privacy class actions, this section details how both subjective and objective harm can present unique challenges in terms of establishing damages and how it may not be obvious how to address and quantify these harms in the context of privacy class actions.

a Subjective harm

Certain types of privacy class action lawsuits involve a type of harm that is more subjective in nature, since it often relates to an emotional or psychological type of harm.[59] This category is usually linked with two types

---

57 Eloïse Gratton, *supra* note 17 at 515; Eloïse Gratton, "If Personal Information is Privacy's Gatekeeper, then Risk of Harm is the Key: A Proposed Method for Determining What Counts as Personal Information" (2013) 24:1 Alb L J Sci & Tech.

58 *Ibid.*

59 In 1972, the Scottish Justice Committee stated that: "(. . .) the notion of privacy has a substantial emotive content in that many of the things which we feel the need to preserve from the curiosity of our fellows are feelings, beliefs or matters of conduct which are themselves

of data handling activities: the collection of personal information and the disclosure of this information.

In their famous article about privacy and the right to be left alone, Warren and Brandeis referred to the disclosure of private facts in the new press, contending that privacy involved "injury to the feelings".[60] William L. Prosser discusses how the common law recognizes a tort of privacy invasion in cases where there has been a "[p]ublic disclosure of embarrassing private facts about the plaintiff".[61] According to Ryan Calo, the subjective category of privacy harm (which is included in the activity of collecting and disclosing personal information) is the unwanted perception of observation, broadly defined.[62] Observation may include the activity of collecting personal information, but this also includes the disclosure of personal information.[63] Calo suggests that many of the harms we associate with a person seeing us, such as "embarrassment, chilling effects or a loss of solitude", flow from the mere belief that one is being observed.[64] Gavison refers to an observation with an "inhibitive effect on most individuals that makes them more formal and uneasy".[65] Recently, in *Jones v. Tsige*,[66] the Court of Appeal for Ontario hinted that there was a subjective component to an invasion of privacy, assimilated to the subjective feelings of "distress, humiliation or anguish".[67]

From the type of privacy class actions that have been filed in Canada in recent years, we note certain cases which would fall into this type of category, because they involve a collection (or an over-collection) of personal information triggering the feeling of being under surveillance. This

---

irrational". Justice Committee on Privacy, "Privacy and the Law" at 5 para 18, discussed in Home Office, Lord Chancellor's Office, Scottish Office (Chairman The Rt Hon, Kenneth Younger), *Report of the Committee on Privacy* (presented to Parliament by the Secretary of State for the Home Department, the Lord High Chancellor and the Secretary of State for Scotland by Command of Her Majesty, July 1972) at 17 para 47.

60 Warren & Brandeis, *supra* note 53 at 197. See also at 198: "our system (. . .) does not afford a remedy even for mental suffering which results from mere contumely and insult".

61 Prosser, *supra* note 54 at 389.

62 Ryan Calo, "The Boundaries of Privacy Harm" (2010) 86:3 Ind L J at 16 [Calo, "The Boundaries"].

63 *Ibid.* Calo states that "So, too, is reading a report of their preferences, associations, and whereabouts".

64 Ryan Calo, "People Can Be So Fake: A New Dimension to Privacy and Technology Scholarship" (2010) 114 Penn St L Rev 809 at 842–48 [Calo, "New Dimension"].

65 Ruth E Gavison, "Privacy and the Limits of Law" (1980) 89 Yale LJ 421 at 447.

66 *Jones, supra* note 4.

67 *Ibid* at para 71. This court mentioned that "proof of harm to a recognized economic interest is not an element of the cause of action", therefore implying that a subjective kind of harm may take place upon an invasion of privacy, even in the absence of an objective (financial) harm.

type of harm often results from a potentially intrusive business practice. For instance, this may include a claim where the allegation is that an Internet service provider inspected Internet traffic,[68] an online web service provider scanned emails sent to its users to send them targeted ads,[69] apps collected and shared information without consent[70] or a technology company designed its product so that it could record and store location data on mobile devices in unencrypted form.[71] The types of cases included in this category may also involve claims where the allegation is that the defendant tracked mobile customers' account and network usage information, including Internet sites they visited to generate marketing reports sold to advertisers,[72] collected location data though mobile phones without users' permission or knowledge,[73] collected call and text message data via mobile phones without users' permission or knowledge,[74] collected unsecured Wi-Fi communications without consent[75] or allowed third parties to access users' personal private information without proper consent through its online social media platform.[76] These cases may also include some of the snooping medical cases, for example, where the allegation is that the defendant was snooping into the electronic medical records of patients for a number of years,[77] accessing the personal health information of thousands of patients[78] or conducting strip searches of 33 forensic psychiatry patients.[79]

Privacy class action cases that may fall into this subjective harm category may also include claims involving a disclosure or a sharing of sensitive information that may trigger a form of embarrassment. These cases may include situations where the allegation is that the defendant, an online platform, used its members' names and images to promote products without their consent;[80] had poor protection measures in place that led to the hacking and subsequent publishing of its online service members' personal names, emails, home addresses and message history of adults in

---

68 *Union des Consommateurs, supra* note 10.
69 *Plimmer, supra* note 10.
70 *Albilia 2013, supra* note 10; *Albilia 2014, supra* note 10.
71 *Ladas, supra* note 10.
72 *Chasles, supra* note 10; *Austin, supra* note 10.
73 *Emond & MacQueen, supra* note 10; *Lima, supra* note 10.
74 *Leventakis, supra* note 10.
75 *Elkoby, supra* note 10.
76 *Thiel & Thicke, supra* note 10; *Chamberlain, supra* note 10; *Leventakis, supra* note 10.
77 *Mallinson, supra* note 9.
78 *Daniells, supra* note 9.
79 *Murray 2015, supra* note 9; *Murray 2017, supra* note 9.
80 *Douez v Facebook Inc,* 2014 BCSC 953 [*Douez 2014*]; *Douez v Facebook Inc,* 2017 SCC 33 [*Douez 2017*]; *Douez v Facebook Inc,* 2018 BCCA 186 [*Douez 2018*].

committed relationships looking for an extra-matrimonial affair;[81] or sent letters to individuals with the text "Marihuana Medical Access Program" on the envelope, therefore disclosing that they are part of the program and are marijuana users.[82]

Given that this type of harm is more subjective, it can sometimes be a challenge to put a price tag on it. This quantifying is also subject to, and depends on, each specific individual and their sensitivity in a given context. For example, following the Ashley Madison incident, a pastor outed on Ashley Madison committed suicide because he was humiliated and devastated,[83] while others agreed to disclose their identity by acting as class representatives in class actions against the company both in the United States[84] and in Canada.[85] Ashley Madison's parent company ultimately agreed to pay US$11.2 million to settle the U.S. class action, while maintaining its denial of any wrongdoing.[86] The Canadian class action is still ongoing, and the class has yet to be certified.[87] It can also be challenging to establish harm that is common to a class of plaintiffs, although the Supreme Court found in *Vivendi Canada Inc. v. Dell'Aniello* that it is not necessary for the whole class to demonstrate "the existence of a common question that would serve to advance the resolution of the litigation with respect to all the members of the group, and that would not play an insignificant role in the outcome of the case".[88]

In the limited cases in which affected individuals have taken companies before the Federal Court after a breach of PIPEDA for a subjective harm (i.e. a disclosure of their information without consent), we note that the amount of damages awarded have usually ranged between $0 and $5,000.

In some cases involving the disclosure of personal information without consent, courts were of the view that no damages were owed.[89] In others,

81 *Shore v Avid Life Media Inc and Avid Dating Life Inc* [*Shore*].
82 *Doe v The Queen*, Fed Ct. T-1931-13 [*Doe*]; *John Doe v Canada*, 2015 FC 916 [*John Doe 2015*]; *Canada v John Doe*, 2016 FCA 191 [*John Doe 2016*].
83 Laurie Segall, "Pastor Outed on Ashley Madison Commits Suicide", *CNN Business* (September 8, 2015).
84 Ashley Milano, "Ashley Madison Class Action Plaintiffs Identify Themselves", *Top Class Actions* (June 18, 2016).
85 Peder Myhr, "Class-action Lawsuit Filed in Canada against Ashley Madison", *Global News* (August 20, 2015).
86 Global News, "Ashley Madison Parent Company Settles Data Breach Lawsuit for $11.2 M", *Global News* (July 14, 2017).
87 See Charney Lawyers, "Ashley Madison Class Action Lawsuit", online: *Charney Lawyers* <www.charneylawyers.com/Charney/ashleymadisonclassaction.php>.
88 *Vivendi Canada Inc v Dell'Aniello*, 2014 SCC 1, [2014] 1 SCR 3, at para 60 [*Vivendi*].
89 See *Townsend v SunLife Financial*, 2012 FC 550; *Stevens v SNF Maritime Metal Inc*, 2010 FC 1137 [*Stevens*]; *Randall v Nubodys Fitness Centres*, 2010 FC 681 [*Randall*].

small values were awarded. For instance, in a few cases involving the disclosure of personal financial information in the context of divorce proceedings, $2,500 was awarded in one case[90] and $4,500 in another.[91] In *Girao* v. *Zarek Taylor Grossman Hanrahan LLP*,[92] which pertained to the disclosure of personal information relating to medical conditions, the court concluded that there was no particular harm but still awarded $1,500 for the breach. In *A.T.* v. *Globe24h.com*,[93] which involved the republishing of an Alberta Labour Board decision concerning the plaintiff on the defendant's website, an amount of $5,000 was awarded to account for the humiliation sustained.

In the medical records "snooping" class action case of *Hemeon v South West Nova District Health Authority*,[94] a rogue health records clerk accessed 700 patient files without consent at a Nova Scotia community hospital, often looking for relatives or patients she knew. The class action recently settled, with each living adult patient class member being sent a $1,000 cheque by regular mail. These cases illustrate that although embarrassment is a harm, it can be a difficult harm to put a price tag on, and the courts have repeatedly considered that it can be worth very little or even nothing at all.

b Objective harm

Certain types of privacy class action lawsuits are raising a more objective type of harm. Calo explains that while at the collection or disclosure level, the corresponding harm may be subjective in nature,[95] the consequence of a third party using data would be much more concrete and, in many cases, would have financial implications.[96] According to Calo, the objective

---

90 *Biron v RBC Royal Bank*, 2012 FC 1095 [*Biron*].

91 *Landry v Royal Bank of Canada*, 2011 FC 687 [*Landry*].

92 *Girao v Zarek Taylor Grossman Hanrahan LLP*, 2011 FC 1070 [*Girao*].

93 *A.T. v Globe24h.com*, 2017 FC 114 [*A.T*]. The judge based his decision on a non-exhaustive list of factors to determine an application for damages under *PIPEDA*: (i) whether awarding damages would further the general objects of *PIPEDA* and uphold the values it embodies, (ii) whether damages should be awarded to deter future breaches and (iii) the seriousness of the breach.

94 *Hemeon v South West Nova District Health Authority*, 2015 NSSC 287 [*Hemeon*]. Settlement was judicially approved in 2017, unreported.

95 Calo, "The Boundaries", *supra* note 62 at 20.

96 For example, when TJX was hit with a security breach, its customers were worried about a potentially costly identity theft. See *TJX Companies Retail Sec Breach Litigation*, 564 F (3d) 489 at 491 (1st Cir 2009) [*TJX Companies*]. In January 2007, TJX Companies, Inc. (TJX), a major operator of discount stores, revealed that its computer systems had been hacked and that credit or debit card data for millions of its customers had been stolen. For Canada, see PIPEDA Case Summary #2008–395, *supra* note 34; PIPEDA Report of Findings #2007–389, *supra* note 34.

category of privacy harm would be the unanticipated or forced use of personal information against a given person.[97] It is often the use of information that leads to a more tangible kind of harm. The Canadian breach notification guidelines and provisions discuss the fact that individuals should be notified in case of a security breach that could trigger a loss of employment, business or professional opportunities, financial loss, identity theft, negative effects on an individual's credit record and damage to or loss of property, which are all harms that would fall into this objective harm category.[98]

The type of harm resulting from a security incident such as hacking, where the third party had access to financial information or other credentials,[99] or the loss of devices containing information that may be used to commit fraudulent activities against the individual,[100] would likely also fall into this category.

Under the recent mandatory breach notification obligation,[101] organizations are required to inform affected individuals of these incidents "as soon as feasible" if there is a real risk of significant harm to the individual in order to allow them to mitigate risks that this information will be misused.[102] Once informed, these individuals can help prevent further harm by paying special attention to their banking statements for unauthorized transactions or being more aware of phishing emails referencing the fact that they are a client of a given financial institution, among other things.

PIPEDA Safeguards Principle 4.7.1 states that an organization must implement security safeguards to protect personal information against loss

---

97 Calo, "The Boundaries", *supra* note 62 at 14.

98 *PIPEDA, supra* note 3, s 10.1; Office of the Privacy Commissioner of Canada, "What You Need to Know about Mandatory Reporting of Breaches of Security Safeguards", online: *Office of the Privacy Commissioner of Canada* <www.priv.gc.ca/en/privacy-topics/ privacy-breaches/respond-to-a-privacy-breach-at-your-business/gd_pb_201810/>.

99 See for example, *Maksimovic, supra* note 7; *Lozanski, supra* note 7; *Karasik, supra* note 7; *Demers, supra* note 7; *Gill, supra* note 7; *Banadyga, supra* note 7; *Drew 2016, supra* note 7; *Drew 2017, supra* note 7; *Zuckerman 2015, supra* note 7; *Sofio, supra* note 7; *Zuckerman 2017, supra* note 7; *Tucci 2013, supra* note 7; *Tucci 2015, supra* note 7; *Tucci 2017, supra* note 7; *Kaplan, supra* note 7; *Azam, supra* note 7; *Ballantine, supra* note 7; *Agnew-Americano, supra* note 7 *Parallel actions pending in other provinces: In BC and SK: *Joshua, supra* note 7; *Thalheimer, supra* note 7; In QC (*Li, supra* note 7). In ONT (*Ballantine v Equifax, supra* note 7); *Setoguchi, supra* note 7; *Fortier, supra* note 7; *Steinman, supra* note 7; *Wilson, supra* note 7; *Levy, supra* note 7; *Marriott, supra* note 7 *Parallel actions in NS: *Mann, supra* note 7; BC: *Krygier, supra* note 7; *Wong, supra* note 7; *James, supra* note 7; ONT: *Schnarr & Brown, supra* note 7; BC: *Sache, supra* note 7; QC: *Won Kil Bai, supra* note 7; AB: *Loveseth, supra* note 7.

100 See e.g. *Lamoureux, supra* note 8; *Condon 2014, supra* note 8; *Condon 2015, supra* note 8; *Condon 2018, supra* note 8.

101 *PIPEDA, supra* note 3, s 10.1.

102 *PIPEDA, supra* note 3, ss 10.1(3), 10.1(5).

or theft, as well as *unauthorized* access, disclosure, copying, *use* or modification. In the Equifax Report of Findings, the OPC discusses Principle 4.7.1 and states that: "In our view, this provision therefore requires organizations to undertake appropriate mitigation measures after a breach to protect against future unauthorized use of the compromised personal information by malicious actors".[103] In that situation, the OPC took into account that most individuals involved had at least their names, addresses, dates of birth and social insurance numbers compromised and that these identifiers combined present a real risk of unauthorized use by malicious actors for identity theft. Therefore, the OPC articulated its view that in this context, it had to examine whether the protections offered to affected Canadians by Equifax Canada were adequate to protect the compromised personal information against such potential unauthorized use over the long term.[104]

In doing so, the OPC took a very broad interpretation of Principle 4.7.1 by extending its scope to post-breach safeguards aimed at protecting personal information. Principle 4.7.1 requires organizations to implement safeguards to protect personal information against "unauthorized [. . .] use". In the OPC's view, this obligation requires the implementation of measures to prevent unauthorized use of the personal information *after a breach has occurred*. In other words, an organization would have the obligation to protect personal information against unauthorized access, disclosure, copying, use or modification when this information is under its control, as well as when it is no longer under its control due to a breach. This position appears to be inconsistent with PIPEDA's Accountability principle (Principle 1), which states that an organization is responsible for personal information *under its control*. This interpretation is also difficult to reconcile with the examples of safeguards detailed at Principle 4.7.3 of PIPEDA, which clearly aim at protecting personal information under an organization's control and do not capture post-breach mitigation.[105] Furthermore, incorporating such an obligation into PIPEDA – to protect information and prevent harm arising from its use *after* a breach has occurred and in perpetuity – would be extremely burdensome on organizations in practice.

Another indication that post-breach mitigation measures are not covered by Principle 4.7.1 is found in recent amendments to PIPEDA,[106] which

---

103 *PIPEDA Report 2019, supra* note 30 at para 148.
104 *Ibid* at para 150.
105 More specifically, PIPEDA provides the following examples: (i) physical measures, for example, locked filing cabinets and restricted access to offices; (ii) organizational measures, for example, security clearances and limiting access on a "need-to-know" basis; and (iii) technological measures, for example, the use of passwords and encryption.
106 These amendments were introduced by the *Digital Privacy Act*, SC 2015, c 32.

introduced an obligation to report "breach of security safeguards", defined as "the loss of, unauthorized access to or unauthorized disclosure of personal information resulting from a breach of an organization's security safeguards that are referred to in clause 4.7 of Schedule 1 or from a failure to establish those safeguards".[107] These amendments would have given Parliament an opportunity to impose a new obligation on organizations to implement measures to reduce the risk of harm to affected individuals resulting from a breach, but such obligation was not introduced. We note that the Breach of Security Safeguards Regulations, which were adopted pursuant to the new PIPEDA provisions, address the information that organizations must include when reporting a breach to the OPC, including "a description of the steps that the organization has taken to reduce the risk of harm to affected individuals that could result from the breach or to mitigate that harm".[108] However, there is no obligation, either in the amendments to PIPEDA or in the regulations, to implement such steps.

Before the OPC's report of findings in the Equifax case, post-breach mitigation measures, such as offering credit monitoring, were taken into consideration by the OPC when evaluating an organization's reaction following a breach but were never considered to be a duty. For instance, in an earlier case, the OPC mentioned: "We also note that the Respondent offered a credit monitoring service to participants affected by the breach, including the complainant. This is an *initiative of merit* that can minimize potential negative outcomes caused by personal data exposure"[109] (emphasis added).

In any event, the OPC's new position is not meritless considering that the purpose of PIPEDA is the protection of personal information. There could therefore be a reasonable argument to the effect that if an organization is in the position to mitigate the risks to personal information resulting from a breach that it has caused, it has a duty to do so. This duty arises in the common law from the application of general negligence principles, as well as statutory principles, including under the Data Protection Laws. In the civil law, a similar duty arises under article 1457 of the Civil Code of Quebec that requires the organization to behave prudently and diligently "so as not to cause injury to another".[110]

This is specifically relevant in the context of class action lawsuits following security incidents when there is a risk of fraud or ID theft. We note

---

107 *PIPEDA, supra* note 3, s 2(1).

108 *Breach of Security Safeguards Regulations,* SOR/2018–64, s 2(e).

109 PIPEDA Report 2014, *supra* note 24. Insurance company overhauls its security safeguards following privacy breach. See also Office of the Privacy Commissioner of Canada, *Mass Mailing Mistakes and How to Avoid Them This Tax Season* (January 2017): "Where Appropriate, Provide Free Credit Monitoring for a Specified Period".

110 Art 1457 CCQ.

that reasonable remedies have in fact often been provided by companies voluntarily in the past as part of compliance agreements or class action settlements.[111] The guidance of the Treasury Board Secretariat of Canada to federal organizations references "one year" of complimentary credit monitoring.[112] In 2014, the OPC considered that a company that was informing customers that a one-year credit monitoring service was being offered for free was showing clear evidence of having implemented best practices to respond to a security incident.[113] While providing 12 months of credit monitoring has been the "common" time-frame,[114] this standard may be evolving. In the recent Equifax case, the OPC negotiated for the company to offer credit monitoring for two years, in addition to the two years already provided since the incident occurred.[115] Following the Desjardins data breach in 2019 that affected the accounts of 2.7 million individuals and involved social insurance numbers, Desjardins initially offered one year of free credit monitoring and then increased that coverage to five years. Ultimately, Desjardins wound up offering free lifetime protection against fraud and identity

---

111 In the Walmart Canada Photo Centre case, the Ontario Superior Court approved a settlement providing that Walmart would pay for one year of credit monitoring services. See *Drew 2017, supra* note 7.

112 See Treasury Board Secretariat "Notification to Affected Individuals: Sample Letter".

113 See Office of the Privacy Commissioner of Canada, *Incident Summary #5 – Life Insurance Company Employs Best Practices in Responding to Mass Mailing Error that Risked Exposing Personal Information.*

114 Nissan offered one year of credit monitoring following its recent breach (case still under investigation by the OPC). See CTV News, "Nissan Canada Informs Financing Customers of Possible Data Breach" (December 21, 2017), online: *CTV News* <www.ctvnews.ca/autos/nissan-canada-informs-financing-customers-of-possible-data-breach-1.3731485>. Home Depot, e.g. voluntarily provided Canadian consumers with 12 months of credit monitoring follow its data breach, and the court confirmed that Home Depot responded in a responsible, prompt, generous and exemplary fashion to the criminal acts perpetrated on it by computer hackers. *Lozanski, supra* note 7 at para 74. There are many Alberta Office of the Information and Privacy Commissioner (OIPC) cases in which the organization offered one year of credit monitoring and the OIPC never indicated that it was not sufficient. See, for instance, the following breach notification decisions: Office of the Information and Privacy Commissioner of Alberta, *Breach Notification Decision P2018-ND-121* (FastHealth Corporation); Office of the Information and Privacy Commissioner of Alberta, *Breach Notification Decision P2017-ND-145* (Sun Life Global Investments); Office of the Information and Privacy Commissioner of Alberta, *Breach Notification Decision P2016-ND-12* (Function Point Productivity Software); Office of the Information and Privacy Commissioner of Alberta, *Breach Notification Decision P2015-ND-80* (U.S. Fund for UNICEF); Office of the Information and Privacy Commissioner of Alberta, *Breach Notification Decision P2013-ND-58* (C.S.T. Consultants Inc.).

115 See *Compliance agreement between the Privacy Commissioner of Canada and Equifax Canada Co* (April 2019) [*Compliance Agreement*].

theft for all of its current and future members, as well as the free credit monitoring already provided.[116]

When reviewing class action settlements in some of the recent security breach hacking cases,[117] it is interesting to note that the amount negotiated in these settlements to account for the damages resulting from personal information being used for ID theft ranges between $5,000 and $7,000 maximum per person and only when an individual can provide evidence that their identities were stolen. For instance, in *Evans v The Bank of Nova Scotia*,[118] an amount of $1.155 million was paid to 165 class members, $7,000 each, who did suffer identity theft as a result of their information being used by the fraudster. The other class members received nothing, since there was no evidence their identities were stolen. In *Lozanski v The Home Depot, Inc.*,[119] as part of the Canadian settlement, the defendant gave $250,000 for documented losses up to $5,000 per claimant. In *Drew v Walmart Canada Inc.*,[120] the defendants paid valid claims for reimbursement of out-of-pocket losses, unreimbursed charges and time spent remedying issues that were traceable to the breach, although the total amount eligible to be received by any class member was capped at $5,000.[121] In *Condon v. Canada*,[122] which involved a lost unencrypted hard drive containing personal information of 583,000 students having received loans under a federal government program, a Federal Court judge approved a settlement in May 2018,[123] providing compensation for any actual loss without cap (but claimants had to demonstrate that they were the victim of an ID theft), but interestingly, the federal government also agreed to establish a $17.5-million inconvenience fund. Each student who made a claim would be paid $60 without a requirement to provide evidence of actual wasted time or inconvenience caused by the breach.[124]

---

116 See "Personal Information and Data Protection", online: *Mouvement Desjardins* <www.desjardins.com/ca/personal-information/index.jsp>.

117 Glaspell, *supra* note 6.

118 *Evans v The Bank of Nova Scotia*, 2014 ONSC 2135 [*Evans*]; leave to appeal certification refused, *Michael Evans & Crystal Evans v The Bank of Nova Scotia & Richard Wilson*, 2014 ONSC 7249 [*Michael & Crystal Evans*].

119 119*Lozanski*, *supra* note 7.

120 *Drew 2016*, *supra* note 7.

121 Any class member making a claim for out-of-pocket losses or unreimbursed charges could receive $15 an hour for up to five hours of time spent remedying those losses or charges if they could provide documented evidence of such losses; if they could not provide documented evidence of such losses, the class member may receive $15 an hour for up to two hours of time spent remedying the losses or charges.

122 *Condon 2015*, *supra* note 8.

123 *Condon 2018*, *supra* note 8.

124 The parties are assuming a 30% take-up rate of the $60 payments, rationalized as compensation "for an average of four hours of wasted time and inconvenience in responding

Some could argue – and the courts have often held – that if there is no objective harm (i.e. financial harm or ID theft) that there is no damage to be compensated even if the individual has suffered annoyances, inconveniences or stress. In the matter *Sofio v. Investment Industry Regulatory Organization of Canada (IIROC)*,[125] while the Quebec Superior Court articulated the view that even if a party cannot prove compensable injury from personal information being used in the wake of a breach, they may claim moral damages as indemnification for nonpecuniary damages,[126] the judge pointed out that the plaintiff's alleged inconveniences – such as having to check his bank accounts regularly – were by and large actions associated with living in a twenty-first-century society. Since bank accounts and credit card transactions are easily accessible by the Internet, it is not unusual to conduct such verifications at several intervals during a month.[127] The court concluded that the damages alleged by the applicant did not constitute compensable injury and dismissed the authorization of the class action against Investment Industry Regulatory Organization of Canada (IIROC). The plaintiff appealed the decision, but the appeal was dismissed and lower court's position upheld.[128]

The Quebec Superior Court recently confirmed *Sofio* when it decided in *Bourbonnière v. Yahoo! Inc.*[129] that the mere fact of being a victim of an incident is insufficient to support a claim for damages. In that case, the court refused to authorize the proposed class action, since the applicant failed to demonstrate the existence of any real prejudice in the wake of a data breach that compromised her personal information. These cases illustrate that claims for damages in these types of class actions may be rejected if it is not possible to demonstrate that the victims sustained a clear objective harm (i.e. fraud, ID theft, etc.).

4 Conclusion

Activities that lead to privacy class actions usually involve the management of personal information: the protection of personal information using adequate security measures (for class actions that relate to security incidents) or the breach of the transparency and consent obligations (for class

---

to the data loss, at average industrial hourly wage rates, net of legal fees": see *ibid* at para 23.
125 2014 QCSC 4061.
126 See para 36 of the judgment.
127 See para 41 and 42 of the judgment.
128 *Sofio, supra* note 7.
129 *Bourbonnière v Yahoo! Inc*, 2019 QCCS 2624.

actions that relate to intrusive business practices). These activities are usually associated with business activities regulated by Data Protection Laws, which have been drafted with flexible and technology-neutral language and are therefore rather vague. Given their flexible construction, it can sometimes be a challenge to determine whether an organization is in breach of its obligations.

Most of the privacy class actions filed in recent years in Canada result from a security incident affecting personal information. Under Canadian Data Protection Laws, organizations must protect personal information that they handle against loss or theft, as well as unauthorized access, disclosure, copying, use or modification. The mere occurrence of a data breach does not automatically mean the organization failed to meet its safeguarding obligation under Data Protection Laws; rather, compliance will turn on whether the security safeguards in place at the time of the incident were reasonable and appropriate in the circumstances. Given the flexibility and the constantly evolving nature of technical standards and what is considered "reasonable" and "appropriate", it can be difficult to assess fault in the context of these types of privacy class actions.

A number of privacy class actions result from an organization having potentially adopted an intrusive business practice. Under the Data Protection Laws, organizations must generally obtain an individual's meaningful consent to the collection, use or disclosure of the individual's personal information. The appropriate form of consent has to be determined in light of the sensitivity of the information (which depends on the context) and the "individual's reasonable expectations". What consumers' reasonable expectations are in any given context, and whether certain activities are legitimate from a privacy perspective, is often a function of many factors, including the social norms that are in place at any given time. These social norms are constantly evolving, and this affects users' expectations. This makes for a difficult and ever-changing landscape in which to determine whether a given business practice was conducted in compliance with the consumers' reasonable expectations.

The type of damages claimed can be very different depending on the type of privacy class action. For instance, the type of damages triggered for consumers after a database of credentials is hacked (which can trigger an objective harm such as a risk of fraud or identity theft), is very different from the type of damage triggered following a situation like the Ashley Madison incident, where a more subjective harm triggered may be a risk of humiliation and embarrassment.

In any event, both types of harm have their challenges. It can be difficult to put a price tag on a more subjective type of harm (such as humiliation or embarrassment), and courts have repeatedly considered that this can be worth very little or even nothing at all. As for the more objective type of harm that could have financial implications (often triggered following a security incident), we note that organizations often mitigate these risks of harm. They may notify affected individuals of a breach incident, which allows these individuals to pay special attention to their banking statements for unauthorized transactions and to be more aware of phishing emails. Organizations may also offer certain types of credit monitoring or identity theft insurance that can further mitigate the risk of ID theft. Affected individuals may therefore have a difficult time demonstrating that they have a valid claim. In fact, in recent privacy class actions resulting from security incidents, certain courts have decided that the mere fact of being a victim of a security incident is insufficient to support a claim for damages and that certain types of inconveniences that arise for a victim, such as regularly checking a bank account for unusual activity following a security incident – especially since this can be done easily online – do not constitute a compensable injury.

Privacy class actions are still relatively new. It will be interesting to see how these cases evolve when they are eventually heard on their merits, both on the issue of the fault/cause of action as well as on the type of damages that may be awarded to affected individuals.

4 *Douez v Facebook* and privacy class actions

*Janet Walker**

1 Introduction

Adjusting to a world in which the reputations of ordinary people are increasingly the subject of widespread public scrutiny and comment is an enormous challenge for all of us. It is little wonder that the legal framework supporting our rights and obligations is struggling to keep up. The factors complicating the necessary developments in the law are myriad, and nowhere are they more complex than in cross-border litigation seeking to vindicate privacy rights with respect to the activities of social media enterprises. The Supreme Court of Canada decision in the *Facebook*[1] case highlighted many of the doctrinal issues to be tackled in the coming years and, in so doing, serves as a good illustration of what might lie ahead in the field of privacy class actions, and more generally, in the field of cross-border litigation.

Among the issues considered in this chapter are:

* the protection of vulnerable classes of litigants from waiver of access to the local courts and the relevance of the practical difficulties that they might face in litigating in distant courts;
* the need to recognize the role of mandatory rules in addition to the doctrine of public policy; and
* whether the nature of the role of courts in regulating businesses operating in the digital economy might need to be reconsidered.

* This chapter is based on the paper "Internet Intermediaries in Canadian Courts: *Facebook and Google*" presented at International Institute of Communications, Canada Communications Law and Policy Conference, Ottawa, November 14, 2017, and at a National Judicial Institute Conference in May 2018.
1 *Douez v Facebook, Inc*, 2017 SCC 33 [*Facebook*].

First, though, it will help to set the scene by reviewing some the features of the *Facebook* case and the Supreme Court decision that highlight these issues.

2 Sponsored stories: "there oughta be a law . . ."

In one of the inevitable missteps of social media giants as they boldly go where no business has gone before, Facebook sought to raise revenue from its 'free' membership service through an advertising product called "Sponsored Stories." This product scanned the pages of Facebook members for their names and pictures to incorporate into advertising to their friends. In members' newsfeeds, "Sponsored Stories" would appear showing, for example, status updates from their friends and photo page posts from pages that their friends had 'liked', which happened to show the products and services that sponsors wished to promote. This advertising was highly cost-effective to the providers of the goods and services, who paid Facebook for it because it did not involve the expense of generating new content and because the ostensible endorsement of products and services by the members' own friends was highly credible.

The flaw in this ingenious arrangement was that none of the members whose names and likenesses had been re-circulated in the advertising had consented to this. It is not necessary to go into the details of the many ways in which the members' privacy was violated in order to understand that this was unacceptable. As an ordinary Facebook member might have observed, it was simply wrong and "there oughta be a law" against it.

Indeed, there was. But before we get to that, it is worth reviewing the course of the litigation that ensued.

a Facebook goes to Ottawa

A class action was brought on behalf of 1.8 million British Columbia Facebook members under a provision of the BC Privacy Act, which grants a right of action in these circumstances.[2] In particular, the Privacy Act mandates the jurisdiction of British Columbia courts "despite anything contained in another Act."[3] This provision was important to the claimants because,

---

2 The *Privacy Act*, RSBC 1996, c 373, s 3(2) [*Privacy Act*] provides: "It is a tort, actionable without proof of damage, for a person to use the name or portrait of another for the purpose of advertising or promoting the sale of, or other trading in, property or services, unless that other, or a person entitled to consent on his or her behalf, consents to the use for that purpose."

3 Section 4 reads as follows: "Despite anything contained in another Act, an action under this Act must be heard and determined by the Supreme Court [of British Columbia]."

although their Facebook membership was free, the claimants had had to register for it and, in doing so, they had been required to agree to resolve their disputes in the California courts and in accordance with California law.[4] The Canadian courts therefore had to decide whether the Privacy Act provisions, ostensibly securing access to the British Columbia courts, or the jurisdiction agreement, ostensibly waiving access to the British Columbia courts, should prevail.

The judges at all court levels had considerable difficulty in converging on a common analysis or result. The motions judge held that the implicit effect of the Privacy Act was to prevent persons in British Columbia from waiving their right to access to the local courts. There were strong public policy reasons for the court to disregard the forum selection clause in the membership agreement and to reject Facebook's submissions that California was a more convenient forum in which to decide the matter. According to Griffin J., the British Columbia Supreme Court had exclusive jurisdiction under s. 4 of the Privacy Act to hear the action, and the plaintiff would be unable to bring her claim elsewhere.[5]

The Court of Appeal disagreed. There was concern that this would give the Privacy Act extraterritorial reach, and in the absence of statutory language explicitly overriding forum selection clauses or evidence that the claim could not be brought elsewhere, the membership agreement should be upheld and the action stayed.

b Two missed opportunities

At the Supreme Court of Canada, the decision was split 3–1–3, with four judges in favour of setting aside the forum selection clause and exercising jurisdiction. The decision confirmed that the exercising jurisdiction where an exclusive jurisdiction agreement has nominated another court is not based on the doctrine of *forum non conveniens*, but on whether or not to give effect to the jurisdiction agreement.[6] This was a welcome clarification of the evolving doctrine on jurisdiction agreements with respect to commercial contracts.

---

4 The Facebook forum selection clause at issue in *Facebook, supra* note 1 at 8, read: "You will resolve any claim, cause of action or dispute (claim) you have with us arising out of or relating to this Statement or Facebook exclusively in a state or federal court located in Santa Clara County. The laws of the State of California will govern this Statement, as well as any claim that might arise between you and us, without regard to conflict of law provisions. You agree to submit to the personal jurisdiction of the courts located in Santa Clara County, California for purpose of litigating all such claims."

5 *Douez v Facebook, Inc*, 2014 BCSC 953.

6 *Facebook, supra* note 1 at 17.

However, for consumer contracts, the result was less helpful. Six of the seven judges chose to endorse the two-part *Pompey*[7] test largely unamended. They held that consumer contracts should be treated in the same way as commercial contracts in the first step, and then the onus should be on the consumer in the second step to demonstrate "strong cause" to set the jurisdiction agreement aside and exercise jurisdiction. The plurality held that in the first step, a "plaintiff may resist the enforceability of the contract by raising defences such as, for example, unconscionability, undue influence, and fraud."[8] It is only in the second step – that of determining whether there is "strong cause" to set the jurisdiction agreement aside – that the nature of the contract as either a consumer or a commercial contract becomes relevant.

At this second step, the plaintiff has the burden. Although the plurality noted that "commercial and consumer relationships are very different" and may entail "gross inequality of bargaining power," the distinction was cast as an interpretive gloss on a consideration of all the circumstances of the particular case.[9] This threatened to cast the law into the "wilderness of single instances"[10] in which the hardship of litigating in the nominated forum would be the focus of the determination. Similarly, subject to considerable discretion was the relevance of the fact that the complaint was a breach of privacy, despite it being described as a "quasi-constitutional right."[11] Treating quasi-constitutional rights as just one of many factors seems unlikely to secure any greater certainty for the protection of the rights at stake than exists for any other rights under a contract. The level of uncertainty was demonstrated by the fact that three of the seven judges in this case were not persuaded that this "quasi-constitutional" right could not safely be left in the hands of a foreign court.

In short, the court's continued adherence to the *Eleftheria/Pompey* strong-cause test, long since left behind in other common law jurisdictions, failed to sharpen the law of exclusive jurisdiction agreements by clearly differentiating their application in the commercial and the consumer contexts.[12] The decision also failed to advance the law on the protection of privacy rights in cross-border litigation.

---

7 *Z.I. Pompey Industrie v ECU-Line N.V*, 2003 SCC 27 [*Pompey*].
8 *Facebook, supra* note 1 at 28.
9 *Ibid* at 38–40.
10 Alfred Lord Tennyson, *Aylmer's Field*, 1793.
11 As exemplified by the language rights considered in *Lavigne v Canada (Office of the Commissioner of Official Languages)*, 2002 SCC 53 [*Lavigne*].
12 The plurality appeared to adopt much of the analysis proposed by the intervener Interactive Advertising Bureau of Canada, whose submissions, apart from a passing reference to one decision from Québec and one from the United States, relied entirely on authorities more than a decade old, long before Facebook was in regular use outside the United States.

These two missed opportunities are particularly significant for online services such as social media memberships. Social media memberships typically involve low-cost or no-cost contracts of adhesion for services that are becoming increasingly central to the lives of millions. Before turning to the protection of privacy rights through class actions, it is worth considering forum selection agreements in both commercial and consumer contracts in more detail to appreciate how the result in *Facebook* was reached and how the law might change in the years ahead.

3 Consumer contracts are different

The majority of the Supreme Court thought that it was time to develop the law relating to forum selection clauses in the context of consumer agreements. Indeed, this question alone would have been well worth consideration by the Supreme Court of Canada, and both consumer and commercial contracts would have benefited if decisive steps had been taken to distinguish the two.

The common law approach to the law of jurisdiction has lagged behind its counterparts in the civil law in providing for the special concerns of consumer contracts. The need for revision has been long in the making.[13] Where international transactions and agreements were once the exclusive concern of sophisticated commercial parties supported by expert legal advisors, the development of Internet communications and dealings has facilitated regular cross-border engagement on the part of individuals and small businesses. As one of the intervenors observed, "[a] test for enforceability of a clause in a commercial bill of lading should not be applied in the same manner to contracts of adhesion that engage constitutional or quasi-constitutional rights."[14]

Unfortunately, the court lacked the doctrinal tools and interpretive framework to develop the law, resulting in a situation in which six out of seven of the judges endorsed the continuing application largely unamended of an unrelated line of cases long abandoned in their English source. How did this happen, and how might the law on consumer contracts in this area be advanced?

a A law without grammar

One of the historical impediments to the suitable treatment of forum selection clauses in consumer contracts lies in a basic misconception in the common

13 See e.g. "Beyond Big Business: Contests between Jurisdictions in a Vertically Integrated Global Economy" (November 2000) *LSUC*, Civil Litigation Forum, Toronto.
14 Factum of the Intervener, Canadian Civil Liberties Association, at 2.

law about the nature of judicial jurisdiction in cross-border cases. Historically, the common law has imagined jurisdictional rules to be trans-substantive and of universal application. In other words, the same jurisdictional rules apply regardless of the kind of case and the nature of the parties involved.

That this is the prevailing view in the common law is evident from the structure of the conflict of laws texts established by Dicey and those inspired by them.[15] The texts begin with several short chapters devoted to discrete topics relating to the analysis of questions of applicable law under a heading such as "General Considerations" or "Preliminary Topics" and then turn directly to the topic of "Judicial Jurisdiction." Judicial Jurisdiction is in no way a particular or specific topic in relation to the "General" or "Preliminary" topics just discussed (which relate to the topics of "Choice of Law"). This is confusing enough, but the confusion is compounded by the fact that as a practical matter, the "judicial jurisdiction" in question is jurisdiction in civil and commercial matters and not in matters such as marriage and divorce, custody and support, real property, etc. This insight emerges only upon careful observation of subsequent chapters on these latter topics and the fact that they each begin with their own discussion of the specialized rules for jurisdiction in those areas. The inaccuracy of the notion of trans-substantive jurisdictional rules is also evident in the statutes governing areas of family law such as divorce,[16] custody,[17] and other areas where the rules of jurisdiction are not derived from the principles governing civil and commercial cases, each of which contains its own detailed provisions for judicial jurisdiction.

Accordingly, the confusion may not come from the textbooks and may reflect some more basic feature of the common law itself; but whatever its source, it is not shared by civil law jurisdictions with legal traditions similar to those in common law Canada. They seem to have no difficulty distinguishing the jurisdictional rules for civil and commercial matters from the jurisdictional rules for other matters.

For example, Title III of Book X of the Civil Code of Quebec (CCQ) concerning the "International Jurisdiction of Québec Authorities" is divided into a chapter for "General Provisions" and a chapter for "Special Provisions." The chapter on Special Provisions is further divided into extra-patrimonial and family matters; patrimonial matters; and real and mixed matters. These categories correspond roughly with family law matters, civil and commercial matters, and matters of succession and matrimonial property.[18] The

---

15 Now Lord Collins of Mapesbury & Jonathan Harris, eds, *Dicey, Morris and Collins on the Conflict of Laws*, 15th ed (London: Sweet & Maxwell, 2018).

16 *Divorce Act*, RSC 1985, c 3 (2nd Supp).

17 See e.g. *Family Law Act*, RSO 1990, c F.3.

18 Arts 3076–3168 CCQ.

Brussels Regulations – the regimes governing judicial jurisdiction in cross-border matters in the European Union – similarly recognize this distinction. The Brussels I Regulation[19] is confined to civil and commercial matters, leaving matters such as family law, in which judicial jurisdiction is based on fundamentally different principles, to be governed by other regimes. Accordingly, in Québec and in Europe, a fundamental distinction is made between civil and commercial cases and other cases, acknowledging that each requires very different connections between the litigants or the case and the forum for the exercise of jurisdiction.

Accordingly, in much the same way as basic grammar tends to be overlooked in the primary school curriculum in anglophone countries but not elsewhere, so, too, has the there been a persistent confusion in the common law on the differences in the logic of the law of jurisdiction between these different kinds of cases.

b Safeguarding consumers' rights, promoting certainty for businesses

In a more specific area of differentiation within the field of civil and commercial matters, the civil law also recognizes the need for special rules for cases involving certain classes of litigants, notably consumers, workers, and insured persons. These rules protect the members of these vulnerable groups from the waiver of access to the local courts through jurisdiction agreements. Article 3149 provides for the jurisdiction of Québec courts in claims based on consumer and employment agreements where the consumer or worker is domiciled or resident in Québec and the purported waiver of the consumer or worker of the right to bring a claim in Québec is invalid.[20] Similarly, articles 17 and 18 of the Brussels I Regulation secure access to the courts of the European consumers' domiciles despite otherwise valid agreements to the contrary.[21]

The Brussels I Regulation defines consumer transactions as those outside one's trade or profession;[22] and a similar definition applies in the common law provinces that have adopted the Court Jurisdiction and Proceedings Transfer Act (CJPTA),[23] although the CJPTA does not protect

---

19 EC, *Regulation (EU) No 1215/2012 of 12 December 2012 on jurisdiction and the recognition and enforcement of judgments in civil and commercial matters* [*Brussels I Regulation*].

20 Art 3149 CCQ; a similar protection exists in art 3150 CCQ for insured persons based in Québec.

21 *Brussels I Regulation, supra* note 19.

22 *Ibid*, art 17.

23 E.g. *British Columbia Court Jurisdiction and Proceedings Transfer Act*, s 10(e)(iii) [*CJPTA*], provides that where a contract is for the purchase of property, services or both, for use other

consumers from the waiver of access to the local courts. To be sure, the distinction between consumer and commercial claims is bound to be contested from time to time as the jurisprudence evolves,[24] but that does not diminish the benefit of this distinction for vulnerable groups. It seems likely that the special provisions in Québec and Europe would have prevented the need for the plaintiffs to defend a challenge to jurisdiction in a situation such as that in the *Facebook* case had it been brought in one of those places.

These special rules also benefit parties to commercial contracts. With the protection of weaker parties secured, it is possible to take a clearer approach to commercial contracts – one that shows a similar respect for party autonomy in forum selection clauses as that currently shown to other terms in commercial contracts. In particular, it becomes possible to relinquish the poorly defined residual discretion found in the "strong cause" test to exercise jurisdiction that has been retained in the face of an exclusive jurisdiction agreement nominating the courts of another forum.

In Québec and other civil law jurisdictions, exclusive jurisdiction agreements are supported by provisions in the law for "negative jurisdiction." These provisions indicate when a court *may not* exercise jurisdiction. For example, in the second paragraph of the article of the CCQ providing for jurisdiction in civil and commercial matters, following a list of the situations in which a court *may* exercise jurisdiction, the article provides that Québec courts have no jurisdiction where the parties have agreed to submit their disputes to a foreign court.[25]

There is no equivalent in the CJPTA,[26] and despite the efforts of some Canadian courts to narrow the scope for the "strong cause" test in commercial cases,[27] there would be considerable benefit in clarifying the effectiveness of exclusive jurisdiction agreements nominating other courts in commercial contracts. Such a provision is found in the Choice of Court Convention,[28] which may one day become the law in many provinces in Canada. In dealing with challenges to jurisdiction agreements in commercial contracts, it is time to relinquish the old English view that "no one by his private stipulation can oust these courts of their jurisdiction in a matter that

---

than in the course of the purchaser's trade or profession, and where the contract has resulted from a solicitation of business in the province by or on behalf of the seller.
24 See e.g. *Dell Computer Corp v Union des consommateurs*, 2007 SCC 34 [*Dell*].
25 Art 3148 CCQ.
26 *CJPTA, supra* note 23.
27 *Expedition Helicopters Inc v Honeywell Inc*, 2010 ONCA 351.
28 The Choice of Court Convention has been adopted in Ontario: *International Choice of Court Agreements Convention Act*, 2017 SO 2017, c 2, Sch 4, but is not yet in force.

properly belongs to them"[29] and instead to rely on the courts' ability, when the need arises, to set jurisdiction agreements aside on the same bases as other terms in commercial agreements.

In this way, improving the "grammar" of the law in Canada would benefit the law relating to jurisdiction agreements in both commercial and consumer contracts. The introduction of the concept of negative jurisdiction would advance the law on jurisdiction agreements in commercial contracts, as would the introduction of special recognition of the interests of vulnerable classes of litigants in consumer contracts.

It may not, however, be sufficient in the case of consumer contracts to consider only the question of access to the local courts. There is a little more to it than that.

4 Privacy class actions: changing times

In the special circumstances of privacy class actions, which serve as a strong example of the current challenges of adapting the law for consumers, there are two other contextual factors, perhaps more obvious than those concerning the grammar of the law, that contributed to the challenges the Supreme Court faced in deciding the *Facebook* case. These relate to two changes to the underlying assumptions on which we intuitively assess the merits of the legal precedents under review.

a Inequality of bargaining power and class actions

The first contextual factor relates to our assumptions about the reasons for protecting consumers from the waiver of access to the local courts. Historically, we understood the considerations primarily in terms of the relative capacity of the parties to litigate in distant courts. On the one hand, we were concerned that the logistical and financial challenges for consumers of travelling to commence claims in the home courts of foreign suppliers of goods or services might preclude them from bringing meritorious claims. On the other hand, we were confident that the suppliers of goods and services were capable of controlling the location in which their goods and services were supplied, and they were capable of reasonably foreseeing the potential for litigation in those places and adjusting their business activities accordingly.

This is the context in which the Supreme Court of Canada decided the landmark decision in *Moran v Pyle* in 1975.[30] The court held that the widow

---

29 *The Fehmarn*, [1958] 1 All E.R. 333 at 335, adopted by the Supreme Court in *Facebook*, *supra* note 1 at 27.

30 *Moran v Pyle National (Canada) Ltd*, [1975] 1 SCR 393, 43 DLR (3d) 239.

of a man killed in his home while replacing a light bulb that was manufactured in Ontario should not be made to travel from Saskatchewan to Ontario to sue the manufacturer for negligence.

In 1975, the hardship of being required to travel to litigate in a distant forum would have been obvious. However, the revolution in electronic communications and the advent of class actions have transformed the context in which consumer claims, including privacy claims, are brought. It would no longer be accurate to envisage individual consumers physically travelling to consult with counsel and to commence litigation in distant courts in proceedings about which little information was readily available to them. To the contrary, the reductions in the logistical and financial barriers for consumers might well be described as an access to justice revolution, reducing, if not eliminating, the barriers to cross-border litigation for members of class actions and, in some cases, for plaintiffs in individual actions as well.

This transformation was foreshadowed in the early 1990s when the British Columbia Workers Compensation Board sought recovery from a number of asbestos manufacturers for the health care costs associated with exposure of British Columbia workers to asbestos.[31] The plaintiff chose to sue in Texas rather than at home in British Columbia in order to benefit from a variety of substantive and procedural features of the law there. And for the same reasons, the defendants wished to defend in British Columbia rather than in Texas. As a result, the tables were turned, and the defendant asbestos manufacturers sought to persuade the British Columbia courts that they were the more suitable courts for resolving the dispute. Each party wanted to have the other party's courts decide the case.

In a related development at the time, the English courts were persuaded that workers exposed to asbestos in mines in Africa were not required to sue in the forum in which the harm had occurred because group actions were not available there as they were in England. Although the House of Lords recognized that the natural forum was the place where the workers had been harmed, the availability of group actions was regarded as a decisive feature in making the English courts more accessible to them.[32] This approach was affirmed this year by the UK Supreme Court in a claim for environmental harm in Zambia.[33]

Accordingly, a question arises as to the Supreme Court's understanding of the mischief caused by a "gross inequality of bargaining power." If it raises a concern about the fairness of the jurisdiction agreement itself,

---

31 *Amchem Products Inc v British Columbia (Workers' Compensation Board)*, [1993] 1 SCR 897, 102 DLR (4th) 96.
32 *Connelly v RTZ Corporation plc* [1997] UKHL 30, [1998] AC 854; *Lubbe v Cape plc*, [2000] UKHL 41.
33 *Lungowe v Vedanta Resources Plc* [2019] UKSC 20.

then it suggests that the inequality of bargaining power could result in the weaker party accepting a dispute resolution clause that was unworkable and would be of no value to it in the event of a dispute. This was evident in the observation of the plurality that "the expense and inconvenience of requiring British Columbian individuals to litigate in California, compared to the comparative expense and inconvenience to Facebook, further supports a finding of strong cause."[34]

This may have been an obvious concern in 1969 when the *Eleftheria* case was decided and the "strong cause" test was developed, and it may even have been relevant in 2003 when the *Pompey* decision was released. However, it seems far removed from the reality of today's world of collective redress. Indeed, the logistical and financial barriers faced by individuals in claims against large corporations today may be no less daunting in the local courts than they are in foreign courts, particularly in cross-border cases.[35]

In short, the harm caused to consumers by accepting the possibility of waiver of access to local courts has less to do with the expense and inconvenience of litigating elsewhere than it does with the importance of local litigation in securing the rights protected. That proposition seemed to elude the Supreme Court. It requires some explanation, but first it is helpful to note a further contextual factor that made the acceptance of the proposition more difficult.

b *Privacy class actions in the digital era*

The second contextual factor relates to our understanding of the nature of social media membership. It is a world that is evolving at an extraordinary pace. Our assumptions about the kinds of persons who use social media and the nature and significance of that use are radically different from the assumptions that we might have held even a few years ago. What we once might have thought to be a casual pastime of the few among us who were highly advanced technologically has become the mainstay of social engagement for a large portion of the population from all walks of life.

Moreover, the costs and consequences of securing a social media member's rights – of access, of privacy, and the like – might once have been dismissed as marginal in light of the fact that there is no charge for membership. However, the personal benefits to members – and the commercial benefits to businesses – are now more widely understood. In 1998, the Ontario

---

34 *Facebook, supra* note 1 at 4.
35 Gerard Kennedy, "Jurisdiction Motions and Access to Justice: An Ontario Tale" (2018) 55 Osgoode Hall LJ 79.

courts showed little sympathy for the proposed plaintiff class with respect to the jurisdictional obstacles posed by a forum selection clause in a claim concerning amounts debited directly from their credit cards for the service "MSN Messenger."[36] The Internet was in its infancy, and the consumers in question were adventurous first adopters paying to explore the novelty of innovative services from young businesses, the most common risk being the unreliability of those services. When this is contrasted with the Internet today as a critical source of timely information, central to the maintenance of the social communities to which so many of us belong and, for better or for worse, playing an integral role in the functioning of modern democracies, it must be acknowledged that the world was a very different place then from what it is today.

And the pace of change in recent years has only increased. Few would regard it likely today that Facebook would make the mistake of offering an advertising product such as Sponsored Stories, even though it must have seemed like a good idea in 2012. Perhaps even more significantly, in contrast with the dismissive approach taken to the importance to members of MSN Messenger in 1998, some members of the Supreme Court regarded the costs and consequences of Facebook membership such as to render it an essential service and one that had the potential to impact *quasi-constitutional* rights.[37]

Accordingly, with the advent of class actions and the rise in the use and significance of social media networks, the necessary impetus to changes in the law is increasing rapidly.

5 Quasi-constitutional rights and mandatory law

Returning to the importance of local litigation in securing the privacy rights at issue in *Facebook*, it is important to recognize that this not as a function of securing access to local courts, which is only indirectly relevant, but instead as a function of securing the application of local legislative policies, which is directly relevant. The plurality in *Facebook* summarized their reasoning as follows:

> The grossly uneven bargaining power between the parties and the importance of adjudicating quasi-constitutional privacy rights in the

---

36 *Rudder v Microsoft Corp* (1999), 40 CPC (4th) 394 (SCJ Ont), 2 CPR (4th) 474.

37 Indeed, in Liam Harris, "Understanding Public Policy Limits to the Enforceability of Forum Selection Clauses After *Douez v Facebook*" (2019) JPIL 50, the author compares Facebook to a public utility warranting regulation in much the same way as a monopoly providing an essential service.

province are reasons of public policy that are compelling, and when considered together, are decisive in this case.[38]

However, the plurality struggled with the lack of "clear and specific language that legislatures normally use to override forum selection clauses,"[39] citing other examples where this exists,[40] and holding that, in the absence of such language, the potential for the clause to impair protection against infringements of "quasi-constitutional" rights was merely a factor in the "strong cause" that a plaintiff would have to demonstrate.

The search for a clear statutory mandate was complicated by the regulatory context protecting the privacy rights in question. Although the rights were important, the legislature had seen fit to secure them only by providing the option of seeking civil redress – and it had not explicitly eliminated the potential for waiver of the right to sue in the local courts. This disconnect was reflected in the result: the Supreme Court determined that the jurisdiction agreement should be set aside on the basis that the rights were "quasi-constitutional," but there seemed to be nothing in the legislation to clarify this. The legislation merely deemed the infringement to be a tort, which would not, without more, distinguish privacy breaches from ordinary negligence.

a The real culprit revealed: PIPA

At this juncture it is helpful to return to the retort that was imagined from Facebook members when they learned that their images had been used without consent in advertising: "there oughta be a law against that." As mentioned, the law that the Supreme Court considered at length in *Facebook* was the BC Privacy Act, notably the sections that create a tort and grant access to the BC court to bring a claim for it.[41]

However, like a true "whodunit" in which the real culprit is revealed to be a character introduced only late in the play, the critical *law* in question was not the Privacy Act at all, but the BC Personal Information Protection Act (PIPA),[42] which was not considered by the Supreme Court. Under PIPA, organizations are prohibited from collecting, using, and disclosing

---

38 *Facebook, supra* note 1 at 4.
39 *Ibid* at 38.
40 *Marine Liability Act*, SC 2001, c 6, s 46; *Business Practices and Consumer Protection Act*, SBC 2004, c 2.
41 *Privacy Act, supra* note 2, ss 3(2), 4.
42 Personal Information Protection Act, SBC 2003, c 6.3 [*PIPA*]. Thanks are due to Glenn Solomon for pointing this out in 2017.

personal information,[43] and they are prohibited from requiring consent to do so as a condition of supplying a product or service, beyond that necessary to provide the product or service.[44] Furthermore, PIPA is stated to be paramount to all other laws, unless expressly exempted.[45]

To be fair, PIPA also does not explicitly override forum selection agreements that deprive individuals whose personal information is misused in breach of the act of access to the British Columbia courts. However, it does make it clear that Facebook's actions were manifestly in breach of the law protecting the privacy rights of its BC members, and it was a breach for which Facebook was unable to seek consent of those affected, regardless of the consideration offered.

At this point, the structure of the regulatory regime in British Columbia protecting privacy merits some thought. While PIPA contains provisions for regulatory enforcement, it relies upon the Privacy Act provisions that deem privacy breaches a tort and grant access to the BC courts to individuals – or more likely, plaintiff classes – to augment the means for enforcing these rights. Although Canadian courts have been slow to recognize the regulatory role of class actions,[46] in the context of privacy rights, they appear to serve an essential function in strengthening the administrative capabilities of the state.

Administrative lawyers sometimes wax eloquent about the variety of circumstances in which the regulatory state operates and the rich diversity of mechanisms fashioned to meet the needs of each. This would seem to be one set of circumstances in which a law that has been proclaimed to be "paramount to all other laws" is provided with a vital enforcement mechanism in the form of a guarantee of access by victims of its breach to the local courts. In this light, the right of access to the courts under the Privacy Act should be understood as no more waivable than the rights granted under PIPA. To suggest that individuals cannot sign away the right to be protected from the improper collecting, using, and disclosing of personal information under PIPA but can sign away the right to seek the statutorily mandated compensation and access to the local courts under the Privacy Act makes little sense.

It is worth noting that this analysis has not relied upon an exercise in characterization of the rights as quasi-constitutional or some other multifactorial

---

43 *Ibid*, s 6(1).
44 *Ibid*, s 7(2).
45 *Ibid*, s 3(5).
46 Janet Walker, "Class Actions Come of Age in Ontario" in Catherine Piché, ed, *The Class Action Effect: From the Legislator's Imagination to Today's Uses and Practices* (Montreal: Éditions Yvon Blais, 2018).

or discretionary test, but merely on an interpretation of the legal provisions themselves in the broader legislative context. However, it is premised on the idea that securing the rights in question depends upon securing access to the local courts – not merely to avoid the expense and inconvenience of litigating elsewhere, which has been discounted as an overriding concern, but to ensure that the laws protecting these rights will be applied.

b Mandatory rules vs. public policy

It is necessary, therefore, to focus not on the loss of access to the local courts per se, but on the loss of protection for the particular rights in question. The Civil Code of Québec provides direct protection of the local statutory rights of consumers and workers in just this way. Consumers are protected from the waiver of protections afforded by mandatory laws of the place of their residence, provided that the products or services that caused the harm were advertised in the place of their residence and the consumer took the necessary steps to acquire them there.[47] Workers are similarly safeguarded from the waiver of the protection afforded to them by the mandatory rules of the law of the place where they habitually carry out their work or those of the place of the employer.[48]

Likewise, in Europe, the Rome I Regulation, which governs the law applicable to contracts, provides that the parties may choose the law applicable to a contract, but this may not have the result of depriving the consumer of the protection afforded by provisions that cannot be derogated from by agreement by virtue of the law which, in the absence of choice, would apply.[49] Elsewhere in Canada, there are statutes that recognize the relevance of access to the local courts for securing the benefits of such remedial laws. For example, franchisees are protected from provisions in the franchise agreement purporting to restrict the application of the law of Ontario or to restrict jurisdiction or venue to a forum outside Ontario with respect to a claim otherwise enforceable under the legislation.[50] And consumers in Manitoba are protected from provisions of contracts purporting

---

47 Art 3117 CCQ provides: "The choice by the parties of the law applicable to a consumer contract cannot result in depriving the consumer of the protection afforded to him by the mandatory rules of the law of the State where he has his residence if the conclusion of the contract was preceded, in that State, by a specific offer or by advertising and the consumer took in that State all the steps necessary on his part for the conclusion of the contract, or if the order from the consumer was received in that State."

48 *Ibid*, art 3118.

49 EC, *Regulation (EC) No 593/2008 on the law applicable to contractual obligations*, art 6(2) [*Rome I Regulation*].

50 *Arthur Wishart Act (Franchise Disclosure)*, 2000, SO 2002, c 3, s 10.

to restrict the application of the law of Manitoba or to restrict jurisdiction or venue to a forum outside Manitoba.[51]

In the civil law world, these laws are described as "mandatory" rules or "laws of immediate application." They are defined in the Rome I Regulation as

> provisions the respect for which is regarded as crucial by a country for safeguarding its public interests, such as its political, social or economic organisation, to such an extent that they are applicable to any situation falling within their scope, irrespective of the law otherwise applicable to the contract. . . .[52]

It is widely recognized that local mandatory rules will operate to displace rules of a foreign governing law, and where they form part of a foreign law connected with the dispute, the court might, in its discretion, apply them despite the fact that local law or some third law otherwise applies to the contract.[53] Examples of mandatory laws include those intended to protect weaker parties, such as consumers and workers.

Mandatory laws are to be distinguished from the notion of public policy, or *ordre public*. In the conflict of laws, foreign laws may be excluded for reasons of public policy only in very rare situations. The standard for applying the public policy exception is indicated in the qualification that foreign laws and rules may be excluded only for reasons of *international* public policy as distinguished from *local* public policy. The measure of the public policy exception has been described as one that affects "fundamental notions of morality and justice."[54] For example, in the period when gambling was still an illegal activity in Canada rather than a regulated activity, the prohibition was supported by a rule that gambling debts were unenforceable. However, it was held that this was a rule of local public policy and did not prevent the enforcement in Canada of a judgment for a gambling debt that had been incurred elsewhere.[55] The very high threshold for the exclusion of foreign law and judgments on the basis of public policy is important because, by its very nature, the conflict of laws entails the application of foreign law,

---

51 *Consumer Protection Act*, CCSM c C200, s 209.
52 *Rome I Regulation, supra* note 49 at art 9(1); Jurgen Basedow et al, eds, *Max Planck Encyclopaedia of European Private Law* (Oxford: Oxford University Press, 2011).
53 European Court of Justice C-369/96 and C-376/96 (judgement of the Court of Justice of 23 November 1999, Jean-Claude Arblade and Arblade & Fils SARL, C-369/96 and Bernard Leloup, Serge Leloup and Fofrage SARL – C-376/96).
54 *Boardwalk Regency Corp v Maalouf* (1992), 6 OR (3d) 737 (CA), [1992] OJ No 26 (QL).
55 *Ibid.*

and an approach that entailed the pre-empting of foreign law merely because it was different from local law would undermine the basic purpose of the endeavour.

c *Mandatory rules and questions of procedure*

In the common law, as with the concepts discussed earlier in this chapter, the distinction between mandatory rules and public policy is not as clearly defined as it is in the civil law, leaving common law courts unsure about the application of mandatory rules. Despite the lack of a clear "grammar" in this area as well, common law courts seem to approach these situations in similar ways to their civil law counterparts.

This is illustrated in the kinds of rules and laws that are described as "procedural" in the common law conflict of laws. It is widely accepted in conflict of laws that the forum applies its own procedural rules. This is obviously necessary with respect to rules relating to the process of adjudicating disputes. For example, common law courts determine the facts of a case based on the examination and cross-examination of witnesses. It would be impractical to dispense with this process in favour of a judge's independent review of documentary evidence merely because the law governing the dispute was that of a legal system in which the facts were determined in that way.

However, the need to apply local rules is less clear in a number of other situations that are said to involve rules of procedure. For example, local rules of priority in insolvency are said to be procedural even though it is not obvious how the application of foreign rules of priority would necessarily disrupt the adjudicative process.[56] Another example can be found in the reaction by some provincial legislatures in Canada to the Supreme Court of Canada ruling that limitation periods were not procedural in nature, thereby warranting the displacement of the limitation period of the governing law with a local limitation period. Following the ruling in *Tolofson v Jensen*,[57] some provincial legislatures passed new limitations statutes providing for the application of local limitation periods in place of longer limitation periods in the governing law. These were said to be responsive to important local policies.[58]

These two examples illustrate the operation of mandatory rules in the common law. This occurs despite the reluctance of common law courts to

56 Janet Walker, *Canadian Conflict of Laws*, 6th ed (Markham, Ontario: LexisNexis, 2005) at c 3.6.
57 *Tolofson v Jensen*, [1994] 3 SCR 1022 (SCC), 120 DLR (4th) 289.
58 Janet Walker, "Castillo v Castillo: Closing the Barn Door" (2006) 43 Cdn Bus LJ 487.

explain their application as a function of the role of courts in certain situations in giving effect to local (public) policy in situations in which different rules (reflecting different policies) might be applied by foreign courts if the matter were decided elsewhere.

6 The limits of comity

On rare occasion, where it has been necessary to retain jurisdiction in order to secure the application of Canadian law, Canadian courts have wrestled with the issue and ultimately opted to do so. Tracking these instances in the jurisprudence is not easy because the reasons in the judgments have rarely reflected this point explicitly. An example from the Supreme Court of Canada jurisprudence will illustrate the challenges involved.

a Parallel proceedings with different equities and policy concerns

In the *Teck Cominco* case,[59] the Supreme Court of Canada had to decide whether a proceeding in British Columbia should be stayed to avoid the possibility of an inconsistent verdict with a related proceeding underway in Washington State. The Washington proceeding was a claim against Teck Cominco for environmental harm arising from historic discharges into a river that flowed from Canada into the United States. The Washington court had welcomed the third-party claim against Lloyd's as a way of securing Teck's ability to pay the judgment. The Canadian proceeding was a coverage claim by Lloyd's seeking to clarify the obligation of Lloyd's to indemnify Teck in the event that Teck was found liable.

The Supreme Court grappled with the question of parallel proceedings and whether deference should automatically be granted to the court first seized. A compelling consideration, although not highlighted in the reasons, was the conflict between the pressing interest in the Washington proceeding in securing compensation for environmental harm and the interest in the British Columbia proceeding in securing a commercially reasonable interpretation of the insurance policy.[60] This conflict seemed likely to produce inconsistent results and to disrupt the ready cross-border enforceability of the judgments that was central to the doctrine of comity fostered in *Morguard*.[61]

---

59 *Teck Cominco Metals Ltd v Lloyd's Underwriters*, 2009 SCC 11 [*Teck Cominco*].
60 Janet Walker, "*Teck Cominco* and thes Wisdom of Deferring to the Court First Seised, All Things Being Equal" (2009) 47 CBLJ 192.
61 *Morguard Investments Ltd v De Savoye*, [1990] 3 SCR 1077, 76 DLR (4th) 256 [*Morguard*].

The *Morguard* ideal, which had been developed in an interprovincial context, sought to relax the jurisdictional standards for enforcing judgments, in part, based on the confident assumption that the result in the issuing courts would, if the courts exercised appropriately restrained jurisdiction, be otherwise acceptable. It is not suggested that in enforcing judgments, the courts would imagine that the results reached in foreign proceedings would be identical to the results that a Canadian court might reach in the particular case. Rather, it was thought that any discrepancy would not be sufficient to warrant refusing to enforce the judgment.

From the premise that foreign judgments should be presumed to be enforceable, it followed that there should be a mechanism to address parallel proceedings, such as there is within Europe where the enforcement of other European judgments is mandatory.[62] However, under the circumstances of the case in *Teck Cominco*, the Supreme Court did not regard it appropriate to stay the local proceeding to eliminate a potential for conflicting judgments and instead preferred to permit the parallel proceedings to continue with the risk that the resulting judgments might have to be refused enforcement in the other jurisdiction.

Similar situations have arisen in other areas, such as cross-border insolvency, and similar results have been reached. Where cross-border cooperation designed to foster a coherent result requires a court to take steps that are inconsistent with local priorities in insolvency, courts have been reluctant to defer to foreign courts, although the analysis in the judgments rarely makes explicit the need to displace the foreign law with mandatory rules of local law.

In one example, a claim against an insolvent Canadian company that had become part of a cross-border group of companies was advanced on the basis of a statutory requirement in the United States affecting the corporate group as a whole. That statutory requirement related to the corporate group's underfunded pension liability. Satisfying the claim from the United States would have eliminated any ability on the part of the Canadian company to meet the other claims made in the Canadian insolvency, which would otherwise have been substantially satisfied, including the pension obligations in Canada.[63] As in other situations, these compelling facts were clear in the judgment, and the result that they made necessary was ultimately reached, albeit through other means.

As with the previous discussion of the characterization of questions as "procedural" rather than "substantive" for the purposes of applying local

---

62 *Brussels I Regulation, supra* note 19, arts 27–30.
63 *Walter Energy Canada Holdings Inc (Re)*, [2017] BCJ No 820, 2017 BCSC 709 (SC).

law, the pressing need to give effect to mandatory rules is met with the concern to avoid taking what appears to be a parochial approach. However, as the world becomes a smaller place, the realities of greater integration highlight the distinctive features of individual legal systems and the policy choices reflected in various areas of the law. Just as priorities in insolvency are based on a complex web of local social and regulatory factors in the economy, so too is the particular balance between freedom of expression and respect for personal privacy and reputation that shapes the law of defamation embedded in the fabric of society.

There are bound to be differences in laws that cannot be fully reconciled or overlooked. These may not rise to the level of moral repugnance as required for the rejection of foreign law on public policy grounds, but neither can they be overlooked. Even among countries with similar levels of regard for the fundamental human rights and with similarly independent and effective civil justice systems, differences in local policies affect the outcome of cross-border disputes. The concept of mandatory rules is a necessary tool in managing cross-border litigation that engages important local policies, even where it means that the results will be different depending on which court decides the case.

b Claiming BC privacy rights in California

In the absence of a concept of mandatory laws, the plurality in *Facebook* struggled with reasoning to support its conclusion that the case needed to be heard in British Columbia. The plurality held that the jurisdiction agreement should be set aside for various factors, including that the agreement was 1) a consumer contract of adhesion,[64] 2) which purported to pre-empt a statutory cause of action,[65] 3) involving the quasi-constitutional privacy rights[66] of British Columbians. The court also noted two "secondary factors" weighing in favour of setting aside the jurisdiction agreement: comparative convenience and expense of litigating in the alternative forum, which has already been considered, and "the interests of justice."

The plurality explained that "the interests of justice" concerned which forum was best positioned to hear the case on its merits.[67] Before commenting on the plurality's concept of "the interests of justice," it is worth noting that the California courts would not have applied the BC Privacy Act. Although the dissent doubted this, it was plain in the language of the

---

64 *Facebook, supra* note 1 at 53–57.
65 *Ibid* at 60–61.
66 *Ibid* at 58–59.
67 *Ibid* at 65.

jurisdiction agreement itself, which provided both that the laws of the state of California would apply and that they would apply "without regard to conflict of law provisions," i.e., without any further consideration of other laws, such as the Privacy Act, that might apply.[68]

Even if it had not been spelled out in the jurisdiction agreement, as the plurality noted, "[w]hether courts in common law legal systems may similarly consider the intention of foreign legislatures, as set out in statutes like the *Privacy Act*, is uncertain."[69] In this particular situation, the right under the Privacy Act would have been displaced by the rights made mandatory by the First Amendment of the U.S. Constitution, as was central to the debate in the *Google* case heard within days of *Facebook* by the Supreme Court.[70] Accordingly, this situation did not entail the risk that a court nominated in a forum selection clause would misunderstand local law, or otherwise fail for technical reasons of pleading or proof to apply legislation such as the Privacy Act. Rather, the California court would have had an overriding obligation under its own law, particularly with respect to the constitutionally guaranteed right to freedom of expression in the United States[71] and the potential for Facebook to assert immunity under the Communications Decency Act,[72] to exclude the application of the Privacy Act.[73]

Accordingly, it was necessary for the BC Privacy Act to mandate access to the British Columbia courts for the simple reason that this is the legislatively established means for securing the rights granted under PIPA.

The plurality avoided dealing with this by holding that, in any event, a British Columbia court was in a better position to decide whether "public policy or legislative intent prevents parties from opting out of rights created by the *Privacy Act* through a choice of law clause in favour of a foreign jurisdiction." Earlier in the judgment the court had expressed a broader hostility to the use of forum selection clauses because they

> divert public adjudication of matters out of the provinces, and court adjudication in each province is a public good. . . . Courts are not

---

68 *Ibid* at 8.

69 *Ibid* at 71.

70 *Google Inc v Equustek Solutions Inc*, 2017 SCC 34 [*Google*].

71 As elaborated on in "Factum of Intervener the Electronic Frontier Foundation" in *ibid*, online: <www.scc-csc.ca/WebDocuments-DocumentsWeb/36602/FM090_Intervener_ Electronic-Frontier_Foundation.pdf>.

72 Section 230 of the *Communications Decency Act*, 47 USC § 230 immunizes providers of interactive computer services against liability arising from content created by third parties.

73 Several amicus briefs in *Google*, *supra* note 70 emphasized the broad implications of the constitutional right to freedom of speech as a concern that would likely compete with the objects of the Privacy Act.

merely "law-making and applying venues"; they are institutions of "public norm generation and legitimation, which guide the formation and understanding of relationships in pluralistic and democratic societies.[74]

This statement reflects an outmoded perspective on international litigation based a view of the role of national courts that hails from a time before the emergence of the broad range of fora, locally and internationally, in today's highly diversified and competitive marketplace for dispute resolution.[75] Parties are free to choose to resolve their disputes through mediation, arbitration, or some other form of dispute resolution and are not required or expected to involve the national courts. This applies equally to the choice to resolve disputes in one court rather than another. There is nothing "unique" about forum selection agreements, as the plurality suggested. The mechanism agreed upon by commercial parties for resolving disputes arising out of their business relationship are but one of the many benefits and burdens that the parties are free to allocate in their bargain.

That said, as discussed, consumer contracts are different. The reason why we restrict the operation of forum selection clauses in consumer contracts is not primarily on the need for "public norm generation" but on the need to ensure that the local courts are accessible as a means of securing the substantive rights that consumers are granted in local legislation. One example of such a right is the right of consumers found in PIPA to be protected from the use without their consent of their names or portraits for the purpose of advertising. This right is not secured by the common law – hence, the need for legislate. Nor is it fully secured by administrative means – hence, the need for a statutory tort actionable in the British Columbia courts and engaging the potential for class actions.

Nor is this right likely to be safeguarded in a contract of adhesion with a counterparty such as Facebook, who is the likely source of the impairment of such a right. The capacity of the legislation such as the Privacy Act to secure the rights flowing from PIPA depends upon securing access to the local courts, not only because, in many courts, foreign law is applied only when it is pleaded and proved to the court hearing the case[76] but also because mandatory rules in other fora may displace the rights found in PIPA.

---

74 *Facebook, supra* note 1 at 25–26 (citations omitted).
75 See e.g. Janet Walker, "Specialised International Courts, Keeping Arbitration on Top of Its Game" (2019) 85 Arbitration 1.
76 This point was amply demonstrated in *Old North State Brewing Co, Inc v Newlands Service Inc* (1998), 58 BCLR (3d) 144 (CA), [1999] 4 WWR 573 in which a British Columbia business was subject to the enforcement of a North Carolina judgment granting relief based

Accordingly, the view that forum selection clauses per se compete with some perceived obligation of a court to generate norms is misconceived, and the court's mention of this as merely a "secondary factor" acknowledges its lesser significance. The underlying reality of this case is that giving effect to the forum selection clause in Facebook's terms of use would deprive members in British Columbia of the rights mandated under PIPA.[77] As Justice Abella noted, this would mean "a clear legislative intention can be overridden by a forum selection clause."[78] Again, while this conclusion was reached by only one of the seven judges who participated in the decision, had the case arisen in Québec, it would have seemed a foregone conclusion of the combined effects of CCQ arts 3117 and 3149, which proscribe waiver on the part of local consumers of their rights under local law and of their access to local courts. The CCQ is a valuable source of guidance in this field.

7   *Morguard* in a post-territorial world

This chapter has considered the ways in which jurisdiction agreements serve to protect the rights of consumers, not by protecting individuals from the expense of litigating in foreign courts, but by securing the application of local mandatory laws through the regulatory role played by class actions. It remains only to make some concluding observations on the ways in which the application of local mandatory rules in privacy class actions and in other emerging areas for claims in the digital era may require us to re-think some of the basic assumptions about the role of the courts in regulating the businesses such as Facebook and Google that are leading the way in the development of key social and economic features of the digital era.

One of the basic aspects of the *Morguard* formulation of *comity* has already been discussed. It has been argued that the vision of a parity of outcomes in civil litigation across the range of cases that enables courts to enforce judgments with confidence, even where they involve non-consenting foreign defendants, fails to account for the need for courts to give effect to mandatory rules of the local law, such as those discussed earlier securing freedom of speech in the United States.[79] Where these rules

---

on rights under North Carolina law unknown in British Columbia despite the provision in the contract providing for British Columbia law. Under basic conflict of laws principles, the law of British Columbia would only have been considered for application by the North Carolina court if it had been pleaded and proved in that court.

77 Now described as a "Statement of Rights and Responsibilities."
78 *Facebook, supra* note 1 at 108.
79 See earlier in s 6.2.

are different in the various fora in which a dispute might be heard, as can well be the case with cross-border privacy class actions, the judgments may well not be entitled to enforcement elsewhere.

Accordingly, another aspect of the *Morguard* formulation of *comity* that may need to be reconsidered in the coming years is the international effect of judicial pronouncements. Historically, the evolution of international jurisdiction has been driven largely by the anticipated recognition of the resulting judgments. In the first edition of his work on the conflict of laws, A.V. Dicey explained the general principle governing jurisdiction as "the principle of effectiveness": a court "has jurisdiction over (i.e., has a right to adjudicate upon) any matter with regard to which he can give an effective judgment."[80] However, where it might once have been thought that the objective is to secure the same effect in another country as the court's judgment has locally, this may fail to account for the current complexities of cross-border litigation, particularly in areas such as the regulation of Internet intermediaries, where privacy laws and other mandatory laws may vary from one place to another.[81]

The results of judicial decisions, particularly in the context of cross-border privacy class actions, are less likely to be immediate or decisive in the way that judgments, for example, in cases of non-payment for goods delivered, might be in local matters. As discussed, the balance between the protection of privacy and the rights of free speech can vary sharply from one country to another. One of the rare examples in the United States of refusing recognition to a foreign judgment for reasons of public policy was in a libel judgment where the issuing court had not accorded the defendant First Amendment rights,[82] and the recently promulgated Hague Convention on the Recognition and Enforcement of Foreign Judgments in Civil or Commercial Matters excludes privacy matters from its scope.[83]

However, even local regulatory action, in which fines are thought to deter by punishing wrongdoing, the prospect for meeting the traditional expectations of the principle of effectiveness seems equally unlikely. For example, when the U.S. Federal Trade Commission, Facebook's local regulator, levied a fine of $5 billion against it in July 2019 for privacy breaches, its share price remained unaffected.

---

80 AV Dicey, *A Digest of the Law of England with Reference to the Conflict of Laws* (London: Stevens & Sons, 1896) at 38.
81 As was considered in *Google, supra* note 70.
82 *Matusevitch v Telnikoff*, 877 F Supp 1 (DDC 1995).
83 *Convention of 2 July 2019 on the Recognition and Enforcement of Foreign Judgments in Civil or Commercial Matters* at art 1(1), online: <www.hcch.net/en/instruments/conventions/full-text/?cid=137>.

However, it would be a mistake to suggest that the cross-border effect of privacy class actions should be measured only in terms of the expectation of the execution of the judgment issued, and where this is unlikely, jurisdiction should not be exercised. To the contrary, the carefully reasoned judgment of a court based on a solid factual record and the thoughtful submissions of counsel can be a powerful tool in shaping public opinion and in informing regulatory developments.

This issue was considered in greater detail in the *Google* decision in which, despite Google's initial willingness to cooperate in the issuing of an order requiring that it de-index a website, subsequently resisted the injunction and then sought and obtained a blocking order against the injunction from a U.S. court.[84] Nor was there a suggestion that the order, even if complied with fully, would be definitive in terminating the viability of the illicit business in question. However, in this world of enormous technological development rapidly creating the potential for enormous harm and for remedying that harm, the capacity of judicial pronouncements to drive the public opinion incentives for Internet giants to engage in responsible conduct in supplying goods and services to the public[85] should not be underestimated. All of this depends upon supporting the role that privacy class actions play in Canadian courts to secure the application of mandatory rules of the law in Canada.

---

84 *Google Inc v Equustek Solutions Inc*, United States District Court, Northern District of California Case No. 17-CV-04207.

85 As illustrated in the pronouncement by the Court of Justice of the European Union in September 2019 on the scope of the "Right to be Forgotten", online: <curia.europa.eu/jcms/upload/docs/application/pdf/2019-09/cp190112en.pdf>.

5 Why class action suits for security breaches need to look beyond privacy concerns

Nicolas Vermeys

1 Introduction

In 2005, hackers managed to gain access to servers containing private data regarding certain customers of TJX, Inc., the parent company of Canadian retailers Winners, HomeSense, and Marshalls.[1] While this was far from the first time a retailer's deficient cybersecurity measures allowed a third party to access sensitive customer information,[2] the media coverage received by the incident,[3] as well as the joint investigation subsequently launched by the Privacy Commissioner of Canada and the Information and Privacy Commissioner of Alberta,[4] seemed to mark a turning point as to how these security breaches – often unfortunately qualified as mere privacy or data breaches[5] – would be perceived from a legal standpoint.

In the years that followed, new legislation,[6] court cases,[7] and investigations into the security measures and practices of Canadian businesses and

---

1 Office of the Privacy Commissioner of Canada & Office of the Information and Privacy Commissioner of Alberta, *Report of an Investigation into the Security, Collection and Retention of Personal Information* (CanLII 41283 (PCC), 2007) at para 17 [Privacy Report].

2 Juliana De Groot, "The History of Data Breaches" (October 24, 2019), online (blog): *Digital Guardian* <digitalguardian.com/blog/history-data-breaches>.

3 See e.g. Jaikumar Vijayan, "TJX Data Breach: At 45.6M Card Numbers, It's the Biggest Ever" (March 29, 2007), online: *Computerworld* <computerworld.com/article/2544306/tjx-data-breach-at-45-6m-card-numbers-it-s-the-biggest-ever.html>.

4 Privacy Report, *supra* note 1.

5 See e.g. Information and Privacy Commissioner, *Investigation into a Privacy Breach of Customers' Personal Information by the British Columbia Lottery Corporation (Re)* (2011 BCIPC 6 (CanLII)); or *Zuckerman v Target Corp*, 2016 QCCS 3160. As will be further discussed in this chapter, by qualifying a breach as a "privacy breach" rather than a "security breach", legislators and decision makers unwittingly limit the breadth of investigations to one aspect of an entity's information security obligations and, therefore, can impact the legal recourse of individuals affected by said breach.

6 See e.g. *Digital Privacy Act*, SC 2015, c 32.

7 See e.g. *Aldo Group Inc v Moneris Solutions Corporation*, 2013 ONCA 725 (application for leave to appeal dismissed in *MasterCard International Inc v The Aldo Group Inc et al*, 2014 CarswellOnt 5661, 2014 CanLII 21559 (SCC)).

organisations[8] have multiplied, therefore giving us better insight into the legal framework applicable to the types of security breaches that now seem to be all too common.

Furthermore, as in the TJX case,[9] many of these breaches have led to class action suits both in the United States and Canada.[10] In fact, a fair number of "[p]rivacy class actions triggered by data breaches" have been filed across the country over the last few years.[11] This statement, while demonstratively true, may seem puzzling to whoever consults the Superior Court of Québec's Registry of Class Actions,[12] since said registry only references three cases in the "Technology, Cybersecurity" category.[13] Although there are probably numerous factors that contribute to this discrepancy, one seems to be the fact that, as stated earlier, many security breaches are approached strictly as privacy issues.[14]

While we would obviously agree that security breaches often have privacy implications, reducing cybersecurity to a privacy concern limits the concept of security breaches as a legal construct (I) which can adversely impact the rights of those who are affected by said breaches and therefore limit the possibility of using security breaches as a premise for class action suits (II).

---

8   See e.g. *Joint investigation of Ashley Madison by the Privacy Commissioner of Canada and the Australian Privacy Commissioner/Acting Australian Information Commissioner* (CanLII 104108 (PCC), 2016).

9   See *In re TJX Companies, Inc, Customer Data Security Breach Litigation*, 493 F Supp (2d) 1382 (Mem) (Judicial Panel on Multidistrict Litigation 2007) and *Wong v TJX Cos*, 2008 CarswellOnt 523, 2008 CanLII 3421 (ONSC).

10   See e.g. the 2014 Target security breach led to a class action suit in the U.S: *In re Target Corp Customer Data Sec Breach Litigation*, 64 F Supp (3d) 1304 (Dis Ct Minn 2014), and in Quebec: *Zuckerman v Target Corporation Inc*, 2018 QCCS 5497).

11   See Éloïse Gratton & Christopher C Maughan, "Superior Court of Québec Authorizes Privacy Class Action in Zuckerman v. Target Corporation", Case Comment (2017), online: *CanLII Connects* <canliiconnects.org/en/commentaries/44655>.

12   Said registry is available online. See "Registry of Class Actions", online: *Registre des actions collectives* <registredesactionscollectives.quebec/en>.

13   *Hong Xin Jimmy Mei v Apple Inc et Apple Canada Inc.*, C.S. Montréal, n° 500-06-000973-194, filed on January 29, 2019; (*Mei c Apple Inc*, 2019 QCCS 4539); *Hugo Langlois v Fédération des caisses Desjardins du Québec et al* (filed on June 21, 2019) Montreal 500-06-001009-196; *Michael Forian-Zytynsky & Elisabeth Prass v Capital One Bank & Capital One Financial Corporation* (filed on July 30, 2019) Montreal 500-06-001012-190. It should be noted that two of these cases were filed after the first draft of this chapter was submitted.

14   For example, while a class action suit was filed following the Equifax security breach (see *Daniel Li v Equifax Inc et Equifax Canada Co*, C.S. Montreal, no 500-06-000885-174, filed on September 11, 2017 and *Li c Equifac Inc*, 2019 QCCS 4340), it is tagged as an "information confidentiality" case, and not a security case even though, as we will see further on, confidentiality is but a subcategory of security.

2 Security breaches as a legal construct

As stated in our introduction, the concept of a "security breach" has slowly permeated through our legislation and caselaw.[15] For example, the Yukon Territory's Health Information Privacy And Management Act[16] states that "'security breach' means, with respect to personal health information (a) theft or loss, or (b) disposition or disclosure, or access by a person, contrary to this Act or a regulation",[17] while the federal Personal Information Protection and Electronic Documents Act[18] defines a "breach of security safeguards" as "the loss of, unauthorized access to or unauthorized disclosure of personal information resulting from a breach of an organization's security safeguards [. . .] or from a failure to establish those safeguards".[19]

While these definitions offer a general idea as to what security breaches are and what their consequences can be, their privacy-centric nature fails to offer an overall understanding of security as a concept. Furthermore, as these definitions are found in privacy legislation, they seem to limit the subsequent obligation to report security breaches[20] to those issues that pertain to privacy concerns, therefore demonstrating the limits of security breach notification legislation.

a What is information security?

As summarised by Peter S. Brown in 1974, "[t]here are really only six bad things that can happen to data. It can be disclosed, destroyed or modified, either accidentally or intentionally".[21] In expanding on this notion, federal legislators chose to impose that security safeguards "protect personal information against loss or theft, as well as unauthorized access, disclosure, copying, use, or modification",[22] an enumeration which, although longer, covers the same basic elements as Mr Brown's definition, yet limits them to "personal information". There lies our main concern with the earlier-quoted legislative definitions of what constitutes a "security breach": Data,

---

15 CanLII references over 270 cases and a dozen pieces of regulation that use the expression. See: CanLII, online: <canlii.org/en/#search/type=decision&text=%22security%20 breach%22%20>.
16 *Health Information Privacy and Management Act*, SY 2013, c 16.
17 *Ibid*, s 2.
18 *Personal Information Protection and Electronic Documents Act*, SC 2000, c 5 [*PIPEDA*].
19 *Ibid*, s 2.
20 See *ibid*, s 10.1.
21 Peter S Browne, "Computer Security – A Survey" (1972) 4:3 SIGMIS Database 1.
22 *PIPEDA*, *supra* note 18, Schedule I, "Principles Set Out in the National Standard of Canada Entitled Model Code for the Protection of Personal Information", CAN/CSA-Q830-96, s 4.7.1.

as a concept, is not limited to personal information; rather, it represents all types of "[i]nformation in a specific representation, usually as a sequence of symbols that have meaning".[23]

Keeping this in mind, and adapting Mr Brown's observation as to the "bad things that can happen to data", we can define information security as "[t]he protection of information and information systems from unauthorized access, use, disclosure, disruption, modification, or destruction in order to provide confidentiality, integrity, and availability."[24] In using this characterization taken from a technological rather than legal lexicon, we can posit that limiting a security breach to the theft, loss, disposition, or disclosure of (or access to) private information is objectionable for two reasons. First, because access to a system, even when the data is secure, could still cause damages and second, because data's availability and integrity are as important as its confidentiality.

These three elements (confidentiality, integrity, and availability), often referred to as the CIA or AIC triad, constitute the pillars on which a security policy is built. Therefore, all three need to be protected against security breaches even though privacy legislation seems to focus exclusively on confidentiality. For example, section 10 of Quebec's Act Respecting the Protection of Personal Information in the Private Sector[25] states that:

> A person carrying on an enterprise must take the security measures necessary to ensure the protection of the personal information collected, used, communicated, kept or destroyed and that are reasonable given the sensitivity of the information, the purposes for which it is to be used, the quantity and distribution of the information and the medium on which it is stored.

While one could suggest that this section covers all three elements of the triad, it should be pointed out that section 10 of the act falls under the title "confidentiality of personal information", therefore leaving out data integrity and availability. That being said, all three obligations stemming from the AIC triad are thankfully reiterated in a number of different dispositions

23 National Institute of Standards and Technology, *Computer Security Resource Center* (last visited 2019) sub verbo "data", online: <csrc.nist.gov/glossary/term/data>.
24 National Institute of Standards and Technology, *Computer Security Resource Center* (last visited 2019) sub verbo "information security", online <csrc.nist.gov/glossary/term/information-security>.
25 Act Respecting the Protection of Personal Information in the Private Sector, CQLR c P-39.1, s 10.

under Quebec law.[26] They are furthermore encompassed in section 26 of the Act to Establish a Legal Framework for Information Technology,[27] which states that:

> 26. Anyone who places a technology-based document in the custody of a service provider is required to inform the service provider beforehand as to the privacy protection required by the document according to the confidentiality of the information it contains, and as to the persons who are authorized to access the document.
>
> During the period the document is in the custody of the service provider, the service provider is required to see to it that the agreed technological means are in place to ensure its security and maintain its **integrity** and, if applicable, protect its **confidentiality** and prevent **accessing** by unauthorized persons.[28] Similarly, the service provider must ensure compliance with any other obligation provided for by law as regards the retention of the document. (emphasis added)

So, what exactly do we mean by integrity, confidentiality, and availability? While legal definitions of these terms are often lacking (confidentiality, for example, is not defined anywhere within Quebec legislation)[29] or do not correspond to their technical purpose (availability is often limited to access, which in turn is usually presented, as in section 26 of the Information Technology Act, as an obligation to limit rather than facilitate availability),[30] technological definitions are plentiful and mostly concordant.

Integrity usually refers to the "property of accuracy and completeness"[31] of data. As the Quebec legislator surmises, "[t]he integrity of a document

---

26 Among others, for confidentiality, see *ibid*, s 10; Act Respecting Access to Documents Held by Public Bodies and the Protection of Personal Information, CQLR c A-2.1, ss 23, 53, 67.2; Act to Establish a Legal Framework for Information Technology, CQLR c C-1.1, s 25 [Information Technology Act]; for availability, see Information Technology Act, ss 19, 23; and for integrity, see Information Technology Act, s 6, as well as art 2839 CCQ.

27 Information Technology Act, *supra* note 26.

28 This obligation implies, *a contrario*, that access by authorised persons must be allowed, which corresponds, as we will see further on, to the definition of availability.

29 We and others further developed this notion in Nicolas Vermeys, Emmanuelle Amar, with the collaboration of Vincent Gautrais, "Le dépôt technologique des documents" (2016) study presented to the Ministère de la Justice du Québec at 85.

30 We and others further developed this notion in *ibid* at 81.

31 ISO/IEC 27000:2018, "Information Technology – Security Techniques – Information Security Management Systems – Overview and Vocabulary" (2018), online: *ISO* <iso.org/standard/73906.html> [*ISO/IEC 2018*].

is ensured if it is possible to verify that the information it contains has not been altered and has been maintained in its entirety, and that the medium used provides stability and the required perennity to the information".[32]

Confidentiality – the component most commonly associated with data breaches – can be defined as the "property that information is not made available or disclosed to unauthorized individuals, entities, or processes".[33] It must be ensured when the information sought, collected, or stored that it is identified as being confidential,[34] not merely when it is personal.[35]

Finally, **availability** refers to the "property of being accessible and usable on demand by an authorized entity",[36] since data, if collected, usually serves a purpose and must therefore be accessible for that purpose. If authorised entities cannot gain access to said data for the identified purpose, then collecting it becomes pointless.

To summarise and expand on the preceding notions, it can be affirmed that a security breach is the result of a voluntary or accidental attempt to affect the confidentiality, integrity, or availability of data or data systems. This reframed definition will, as we shall now see, affect how we should address data breach notifications.

b The limits of security breach notification legislation

Now that we possess a common lexicon as to what constitutes information security and, moreover, security breaches, we can address how the handling of these breaches is approached by the legislative branch. While liability legislation undoubtedly applies to the damages suffered following a security breach,[37] from a pragmatic standpoint, damages can only be claimed if a series of events happen:

- The breach must be discovered. This may seem obvious, but the fact is that many security breaches remain unnoticed for prolonged periods of time.[38] For example, the TJX breach was discovered more than

---

32 *Information Technology Act, supra* note 26, s 6.
33 ISO/IEC 2018, *supra* note 31.
34 *Information Technology Act, supra* note 26, s 25.
35 The French version of the Information Technology Act, *supra* note 26, s 20, makes a clear distinction between confidential and personal information, as does the Public Health Act, CQLR c S-2.2, s 95.
36 ISO/IEC 2018, *supra* note 31.
37 For more on this issue, see Nicolas Vermeys, *Responsabilité civile et sécurité informationnelle* (Cowansville, QC: Yvon Blais, 2010) at 101.
38 Privacy Report, *supra* note 1 at para 5.

15 months after it happened.[39] While the current mean time to identify a breach is much shorter (197 days, according to one reputable source),[40] it remains relatively long for someone whose information is being accessed by a third party.

- The breach must be disclosed; otherwise, the victim will be unaware of his or her rights.
- The breach must be linked to the damages suffered by the victim (such as identity theft).[41] While causation is a basic component of liability regimes,[42] this might constitute an issue, since confidential data is commonly shared with more than one party, making the source of a leak often difficult to identify.[43]

Enter security breach notification laws, i.e. "legislation requiring private or governmental entities to notify individuals of security breaches of information involving personally identifiable information".[44] While these laws have been around for years in the United States[45] and Europe,[46] the obligation to disclose security breaches first made its way into Canadian legislation in 2009 through Alberta's Personal Information Protection Act.[47] According to section 34.1 of the act:

> An organization having personal information under its control must, without unreasonable delay, provide notice to the Commissioner of any incident involving the loss of or unauthorized access to or disclosure of the personal information where a reasonable person would consider that there exists a real risk of significant harm to an individual as a result of the loss or unauthorized access or disclosure.

---

39 *Ibid* at paras 90–92.
40 IBM, "2018 Cost of a Data Breach Study: Global Overview" (2018), online: *IBM Security* <databreachcalculator.mybluemix.net/>.
41 Privacy Report, *supra* note 1 at para 43.
42 Art 1457 CCQ.
43 For a deeper analysis of this concept, see Nicolas Vermeys, "Fostering Trust and Confidence in Electronic Commerce: Will the EU-Canada Comprehensive Economic and Trade Agreement Really Effect Change?" (2015) 20:2 Lex Electronica 63 at 81 [Vermeys, "Trust and Confidence in Electronic Commerce"].
44 National Conference of State Legislatures, "Security Breach Notification Laws" (September 29, 2019), online: *National Conference of State Legislatures* <www.ncsl.org/research/telecommunications-and-information-technology/security-breach-notification-laws.aspx>.
45 *Ibid.*
46 See Vermeys, "Trust and Confidence in Electronic Commerce", *supra* note 43 at 82–83.
47 Personal Information Protection Act, SA 2003, c P-6.5 [PIPA].

In 2018, a similar disposition added to PIPEDA through the Digital Privacy Act[48] came into effect:

10.1(1) An organization shall report to the Commissioner any breach of security safeguards involving personal information under its control if it is reasonable in the circumstances to believe that the breach creates a real risk of significant harm to an individual.

(2) The report shall contain the prescribed information and shall be made in the prescribed form and manner as soon as feasible after the organization determines that the breach has occurred.

(3) Unless otherwise prohibited by law, an organization shall notify an individual of any breach of security safeguards involving the individual's personal information under the organization's control if it is reasonable in the circumstances to believe that the breach creates a real risk of significant harm to the individual.

(4) The notification shall contain sufficient information to allow the individual to understand the significance to them of the breach and to take steps, if any are possible, to reduce the risk of harm that could result from it or to mitigate that harm. It shall also contain any other prescribed information.

(5) The notification shall be conspicuous and shall be given directly to the individual in the prescribed form and manner, except in pre-scribed circumstances, in which case it shall be given indirectly in the prescribed form and manner.

(6) The notification shall be given as soon as feasible after the organization determines that the breach has occurred.

(7) For the purpose of this section, significant harm includes bodily harm, humiliation, damage to reputation or relationships, loss of employment, business or professional opportunities, financial loss, identity theft, negative effects on the credit record and damage to or loss of property.

(8) The factors that are relevant to determining whether a breach of security safeguards creates a real risk of significant harm to the individual include:

(a) the sensitivity of the personal information involved in the breach;

(b) the probability that the personal information has been, is being or will be misused; and

(c) any other prescribed factor.

---

48 *Digital Privacy Act, supra* note 6.

But, as stated earlier, security breaches do not only impact the confidentiality of private information. They can also affect sensitive data relating to corporations or public bodies. Quebec legislators seemed to understand this important concept when they drafted what would become section 25 of the Information Technology Act. As per this section:

> 25. The person responsible for access to a technology-based document containing confidential information must take appropriate security measures to protect its confidentiality, such as controlling access to the document by means of a restricted view technique, or any technique that prevents unauthorized persons from accessing such information or from otherwise accessing the document or the components providing access to the document.

By addressing confidential rather than private information, this disposition allows for security breach suits (class action or otherwise) that affect more than privacy concerns.

However, as we stated earlier, confidentiality is not the only thing at risk when a security breach occurs. The availability and integrity of data and infrastructures must also be considered, since the destruction or modification of data by a third party could, in certain cases, cause harm, yet not require reporting under the Personal Information Protection Act (PIPA) or Personal Information Protection and Electronic Documents Act (PIPEDA). For example, in *Kochar* v. *University of Saskatchewan*,[49] it is explained that Mr Kochar hacked into his university's system to modify his grades. While this constitutes a criminal offence[50] for which Mr Kochar was convicted, and while the university most definitely suffered a security breach, said breach caused no harm to Mr Kochar – the person whose personal information was accessed. Therefore, notifying Mr Kochar, as required under section 10.1(3) of PIPEDA, "of any breach of security safeguards involving [his] personal information" would be pointless. The true victims of this breach are the potential employers that would have relied on Mr Kochar's doctored grades. Unfortunately, informing these individuals of the breach would have arguably been extremely complex, if not unfeasible (asking an organisation – in this case the university – to notify an almost infinite number of third parties seems unreasonable) unless said employers contacted the university to enquire about Mr Kochar.

---

49 *Kochar v University of Saskatchewan* (1998), [1999] 3 WWR 531, 169 Sask R 119 (SKQB) [*Kochar*].
50 *Criminal Code*, RSC 1985, c C-46, s 430(1.1).

While the *Kochar* case is a peculiar and unique one, it does serve to demonstrate the narrow impact of PIPA and PIPEDA's breach notification dispositions, since they only serve to inform third parties whose personal information is at risk of confidentiality breaches relating to said information and ignore all other aspects of information security, therefore failing to consider the potential interest of third parties in the integrity of data.

3   Security breaches as a premise for class action suits

As stated earlier, under PIPEDA, security breaches need only be disclosed if they affect personal information,[51] and only if the breach creates a real risk of significant harm to the individual to whom the information belongs.[52] Therefore, extending notification obligations to security breaches involving other types of data would either require substantial amendments to PIPEDA and its scope or the adoption of new legislation. As there is – to our knowledge – no current government intent to follow either of these roads, we are left with a system that only imposes notification if a security breach affects personal data. As discussed, this may cause issues, since such a narrow view of when data breaches should be reported to the public will limit the capacity of those affected by said breaches to take precautions and, if need be, legal recourse against the company or organisation whose lax security policies have allowed the breach to happen in the first place.

That being said, even if a company reports a security breach, those affected by said breach still face an uphill climb, since, as we will now address, class action suits for security breaches must meet evidentiary burdens that are often unattainable. This is why we believe that lawyers need to rethink how they approach security breach liability issues, since it remains improbable that the legislator will do so anytime soon.

a   The problem with class action suits for security breaches

As is well established,[53] in Quebec, in order for a class action suit to be authorised, the proposed group representative must demonstrate that:

---

51 Although it somewhat goes without saying, PIPEDA, *supra* note 18, ss 10.1–10.3 are found in Part 1 of the act (Protection of Personal Information in the Private Sector), and not in Part 2 (Electronic Documents). These dispositions can therefore only be applied to data breaches affecting personal information, which implies that all other breaches are exempt from their application.

52 See PIPEDA, *supra* note 18, ss 10.1–10.3.

53 See *L'Oratoire Saint-Joseph du Mont-Royal v J.J.*, 2019 SCC 35 [*L'Oratoire Saint-Joseph*].

- the claims of the members of the class raise identical, similar, or related issues of law or fact;
- the facts alleged appear to justify the conclusions sought;
- the composition of the class makes it difficult or impracticable to apply the rules for mandates to take part in judicial proceedings on behalf of others or for consolidation of proceedings; and
- the class member appointed as representative plaintiff is in a position to properly represent the class members.[54]

With regard to security breaches, when they are reduced to mere privacy breaches, "although the applicant's burden is not onerous and what must be met is a minimum threshold",[55] it remains somewhat difficult to establish a "colour of right", i.e. to meet the second criteria listed earlier.[56] There are two reasons that explain this observation. The first is that it is extremely difficult to establish damages in a privacy breach unless one can prove that their private information has been used for the purposes of identity theft, extorsion, or other illicit activities. The second is that, as we eluded to earlier, causality in data breach cases remains difficult to ascertain.

While we obviously do not condone the authorisation of a class should no real damages exist, we would posit that the evidentiary threshold, as well as the current financial awards associated with class action suits revolving around security breaches, offer no real incentives for companies and organisations to secure their clients' data. Although higher fines could encourage the adoption of stronger security measures and policies, current legislation falls short of giving the Privacy Commissioner of Canada or his provincial counterparts sufficient leeway to properly penalise negligent actors.[57] Therefore, if consumers are to suffer the consequences of legislative tepidity, their legal representatives need to better exploit the legislative tools at their disposal, which implies going beyond privacy concerns. Limiting oneself to the privacy route could also prove to be a disservice to members of a class, as their real damages (which will often extend further than privacy concerns) could be ignored further down the line.

---

54 Art 575 CCP.
55 *L'Oratoire Saint-Joseph, supra* note 53 at para 110.
56 See e.g. *Sofio c Organisme canadien de réglementation du commerce des valeurs mobilières (OCRCVM)*, 2014 QCCS 4061 (confirmed on appeal: *Sofio c Organisme canadien de réglementation du commerce des valeurs mobilières (OCRCVM)*, 2015 QCCA 1820).
57 For example, as per PIPEDA, *supra* note 18, s 28, the maximum fine for not reporting a security breach is limited to $100,000. For big corporations, this amount is minimal when compared to the costs of maintaining a secure infrastructure.

i The difficulty in establishing damages

As we just stated, it is somewhat difficult to establish damages regarding a privacy breach unless a crime[58] is committed using one's data. Otherwise, while "it is not necessary in a data loss case for the petitioner to allege that he or she has been the victim of fraud or identity theft",[59] the fact remains that damages which fall "squarely within the field of 'speculation' and 'unverified hypotheses' [. . .] ought not be considered in assessing whether there is a *prima facie* existence of damages".[60]

Numerous factors justify such a conclusion. For example, data might have fallen into the wrong hands, but the culprit may not have any interest or use for it. Furthermore, in certain cases, he or she may be caught before the data can be monetized. Finally, data may be lost (and therefore unavailable), but not necessarily compromised. This was the case in *Condon* v. *Canada*:[61]

> In November 2012, the Minister [of Human Resources and Skills Development Canada] lost an external hard drive on which it had stored the personal information of the Plaintiffs as well as approximately 583,000 individuals [the Hard Drive], from its offices in Gatineau, Quebec [the Data Loss]. This personal information included the names, dates of birth, addresses, student loan balances, and Social Insurance Numbers [the SIN(s)] of those individuals [the Personal Information]. The Hard Drive has not been recovered.[62]

While it was established that "[t]he information on the Hard Drive was not encrypted, nor was the Hard Drive stored in a location that was locked '100% of the time'",[63] there is no evidence as to who took the drive and what he or she planned to do with it. For all we know, the drive could have been mistakenly discarded and is currently in a landfill, or it could have been stolen by someone who then formatted the drive to use it to back up their own data, therefore creating no real privacy concerns for Mr Condon. For these and other reasons, the court found that a claim based on this issue would fail. As the court explains:

---

58 Privacy Report, *supra* note 1 at para 77.
59 *Zuckerman v Target Corporation*, 2017 QCCS 110 at para 69 [*Zuckerman 2017*].
60 *Mazzonna v DaimlerChrysler Financial Services Canada Inc*, 2012 QCCS 958 at para 66 [*Mazzonna*].
61 *Condon v Canada*, 2014 FC 250 [*Condon 2014*].
62 *Ibid* at para 2.
63 *Ibid* at para 9.

a summary review of the evidence adduced by both parties leads the Court to the conclusion that the Plaintiffs have not suffered any compensable damages. The Plaintiffs have not been victims of fraud or identity theft, they have spent at most some four hours over the phone seeking status updates from the Minister, they have not availed themselves of any credit monitoring services offered by the credit reporting agencies nor have they availed themselves of the Credit Flag service offered by the Defendant.[64]

It should be noted that this conclusion was successfully appealed because the plaintiffs also claimed to have suffered "'costs incurred in preventing identity theft' and 'out-of-pocket expenses'"[65] and that the case was eventually settled out of court.[66] However, it remains doubtful that damages such as "wasted-time, inconvenience, frustration and anxiety resulting from the Data Loss"[67] would give rise to an award, since, as stated in *Mustapha* v. *Culligan of Canada Ltd.*,[68] "[t]he law does not recognize upset, disgust, anxiety, agitation or other mental states that fall short of injury".[69] The court in *Mustapha* goes on to specify:

> I would not purport to define compensable injury exhaustively, except to say that it must be serious and prolonged and rise above the ordinary annoyances, anxieties and fears that people living in society routinely, if sometimes reluctantly, accept.[70]

Not only is this threshold difficult to meet, it also underscores the fact that, in many cases, no substantial damages will be suffered if individuals choose to deal with "ordinary annoyances" like "the monitoring of bank accounts

---

64 *Ibid* at para 68. It should be pointed out that the class was still certified following other considerations.

65 *Condon v Canada*, 2015 FCA 159 at para 22.

66 *Condon v Canada*, 2018 FC 522.

67 *Condon 2014, supra* note 61 at para 65. See also *Zuckerman 2017, supra* note 59 at para 69: "it is not necessary in a data loss case for the petitioner to allege that he or she has been the victim of fraud or identity theft. Other damages may be sufficient, but there must be something more than a mere allegation of stress and of taking routine steps".

68 *Mustapha v Culligan of Canada Ltd*, 2008 SCC 27 [*Mustapha*]. While this case was decided under common law, "the distinction described by the Supreme Court is applicable in Québec". See *Zuckerman 2017, supra* note 59 at para 66. See also *Mazzonna, supra* note 60 at para 61.

69 *Mustapha, supra* note 68 at para 9.

70 *Ibid.*

and credit cards".[71] Granted, it was also decided that "setting up credit monitoring and security alerts, obtaining credit reports, and cancelling cards or closing accounts and replacing them are not 'ordinary annoyances, anxieties and fears that people living in society routinely, if sometimes reluctantly, accept'",[72] but the amounts awarded for these "serious and prolonged" annoyances remain small.

Coupling this observation with the fact that art 1479 of the Quebec Civil Code (CCQ) reminds us that "[a] person who is bound to make reparation for an injury is not liable for any aggravation of the injury that the victim could have avoided" leads us to suggest that even a successful class action suit pertaining to a privacy breach will wield underwhelming results,[73] and this isn't even considering the low value that has historically been attributed to private information.[74]

ii The difficulty in establishing causality

As previously mentioned, another reason class actions for security breaches are often doomed to fail is the fact that the plaintiffs will need to demonstrate causality between the breach and the damages they suffered.[75] After all, as we stated elsewhere,[76] since individuals – be it private citizens, corporations, or public bodies – share their data with numerous third parties (webmail services, social networks, Internet service providers, financial institutions, online merchants, etc.), it becomes difficult, if not simply unfeasible, to establish which organisation's possible security breach could be responsible for confidential or otherwise sensitive information being accessed and used by a malevolent third party.

In other words, just because a corporation suffers a security breach doesn't mean that it is responsible for a person's data being used by a third

71 *Zuckerman 2017, supra* note 59 at para 72.
72 *Ibid.*
73 For example, the settlement in *Lozanski v Home Depot, Inc*, 2016 ONSC 5447 [*Lozanski*] was of approximately $400,000 to be split among 500,000 class members.
74 Studies show that awards for privacy violations are often financially conservative. See Karl Delwaide & Antoine Aylwin, *Leçons tirées de dix ans d'expérience: la Loi sur la protection des renseignements personnels dans le secteur privé du Québec* (Ottawa: Commissaire à la protection de la vie privée du Canada, 2005) at 165. It must, however, be noted that there are important exceptions to this rule, as in *Veilleux c Compagnie d'assurance-vie Penncorp*, 2008 QCCA 257 [*Veilleux*], where the Quebec Court of Appeal awarded $125,000 in damages for privacy violations.
75 Art 1457 CCQ.
76 We explored some of these ideas in a previous paper. See Vermeys, "Trust and Confidence in Electronic Commerce", *supra* note 43 at 81.

party. While data security breach notification laws create a presumption of provenance in the victim's mind, it should not give way to a legal presumption of causality. This is not to say that notification laws do not serve a purpose – it is important for individuals to know their information is at risk to allow them to cancel credit cards or change passwords – but that purpose is not necessarily linked to getting restitution for damages suffered.

For example, a survey of the most important security breaches of 2018 lists a series of companies such as Google, Facebook, Marriott, British Airways, etc., whose systems were accessed by hackers.[77] As most individuals have shared data with at least two or more of these corporations, how can the true liable party be identified should one of their customers be the victim of identity theft? In the same vein, class action suits were filed against Target and Home Depot for similar data breaches that happened within a few months from one another. The Home Depot class was described as "[a]ll persons in Canada, who, between April 11, 2014 and September 13, 2014, made a purchase at a Home Depot store using a credit card or debit card at a self-checkout terminal",[78] while the Target class included "[a]ll persons in Quebec whose payment card data and/or personal information was lost by and/or stolen from Respondent as a result of the data breach that occurred between at least November 27, 2013 and December 15, 2013".[79] It is highly plausible that fractions of these two classes intersect, making it difficult for a victim of credit card fraud who shopped at both establishments during that time frame to know which security breach was responsible for his or her situation.

Granted, CCQ art 1480 could be used to resolve that issue. As a reminder, this disposition states that

> [w]here several persons [. . .] have committed separate faults each of which may have caused the injury, and where it is impossible to determine [. . .] which of them actually caused the injury, they are solidarily bound to make reparation therefor.[80]

In this case, as both companies are claimed to have failed to secure their customers' data, it could be argued that they committed separate faults, either of which could have allowed the subsequent identity theft. However,

---

77 Paige Leskin, "The 21 Scariest Data Breaches of 2018" (December 30, 2018), online: *Business Insider* <www.businessinsider.com/data-hacks-breaches-biggest-of-2018-2018-12>.
78 *Lozanski, supra* note 73 at para 18.
79 *Zuckerman 2017, supra* note 59 at para 131.
80 It should be noted that this same principle can be found under common law. See *Cook v Lewis*, [1951] SCR 830, [1952] 1 DLR 1.

since breaches are rarely identified and declared in a prompt manner, the faulty party may be one that has yet to identify its breach. Furthermore, while CCQ art 1480 creates a reversal of the burden of proof,[81] such burden is alleviated, as we saw earlier, by CCQ art 1479, since it forces the victim to take the necessary precautions to limit his or her damages.

For the previously stated reasons, while privacy laws remain the main vehicle for claims regarding security breaches, they offer a somewhat unsatisfactory solution for claimants because of the difficulties surrounding the establishment of damages and a causal link. For these reasons, as we will now address, it may be beneficial to approach security breaches in a more holistic manner when considering class action suits pertaining to said breaches.

b How to rethink security breach liability

In 2004, the Royal Bank of Canada (RBC) fell victim to a "computer failure"[82] that paralysed its infrastructure for a number of days.[83] In this particular case, the failure was not the result of a malicious hacker exploiting a vulnerability in the bank's system, but rather the consequence of "a single worker entering 'a relatively small number' of incorrect pieces of code into key banking software".[84] That being said, while the cause of the computer failure was a good-faith mistake, the outcome remained the same: bank customers were left unable to access their bank statements and to withdraw funds. This is a perfect example of the accidental exploitation of a system vulnerability that affects the availability of information and, therefore, that constitutes a security breach. However, the RBC breach was not treated as such because "its customers' money was protected and secure"[85] [translation]. Furthermore, as the private information of the bank's customers was not affected, this did not trigger an investigation by the Privacy Commissioner.

Our observations may seem rhetorical, given that a class action suit was authorised[86] and later settled out of court.[87] Yet we would argue that had this

---

81 *St-Jean v Mercier*, [2002] 1 SCR 491 at para 118, 209 DLR (4th) 513.
82 *Bergeron c Banque Royale du Canada*, 2006 QCCS 5226 at para 7 [*RBC*].
83 John Saunders & Paul Waldie, "Human Error Caused Massive RBC Glitch, Officials Concedes" (June 10, 2004, last updated April 20, 2018), online: *The Globe and Mail* <www.theglobeandmail.com/report-on-business/human-error-caused-massive-rbc-glitch-official-concedes/article1000439/>.
84 *Ibid.*
85 *Bergeron, supra* note 82 at para 10.
86 *Ibid* at para 91.
87 *Option Consommateurs c Banque Royale*, 2009 QCCS 4485.

case been treated as a security breach rather than a "computer failure", the legal ramifications might have been different.

In fact, we would dispute the claim that "its customers' money was protected and secure"[88] [translation]. The money was "secure" only in the sense that it could not be accessed by unauthorised persons. However, it also could not be accessed by authorised people, which was the main issue. Furthermore, as "being secure" refers to being "free from risk or loss",[89] we would argue that the data (what was inaccessible was bank information – the material money was there) was not secure, as there was a risk (however slim) of it being unrecoverable.

This is not to say that we would choose to criticise the outcome of the RBC case or, for that matter, of any of the cases we referred to in this chapter. We would simply argue that they share a common trait: approaching only one aspect of security while ignoring the others. For example, if the fear of your data being used to commit identity theft usually won't be recognised as a valid form of prejudice,[90] being unable to rely on data because it was not secured could be. After all, since a technological document's validity and worth will be dependent on its integrity,[91] being unable to establish said integrity because a third party illegally accessed the document could, in certain cases, be a valid cause for action.

We are not suggesting that those representing claimants in a class action suit pile on the arguments (including those put forth in this chapter) if they do not apply to the case at hand. However, a novel approach based on the different legal obligations stemming from the AIC triad might afford a better shot at success – especially at the authorisation stage. For example, in the *Condon* case, "the Plaintiffs allege[d] that the Defendant committed the following breaches of the Contracts:"[92]

- Failure to adhere to the standards for the protection of Personal Information, as set out in the statutes that are expressly referred to in the Contracts;
- Failure to adhere to the Minister's policies;
- Disclosure of Personal Information in a manner not permitted under the Contracts;
- Failure to destroy the Personal Information in the manner required by the Contracts:

88 *RBC, supra* note 82 at para 10.
89 Merriam Webster, *Dictionary* (2019) sub verbo "secure", online: <merriam-webster.com/dictionary/secure>.
90 *Mazzonna, supra* note 60 at para 66.
91 See Information Technology Act, *supra* note 26, s 5.
92 *Condon 2014, supra* note 61 at para 47.

- Retention of the Personal Information for a period longer than allowed under the terms of the Contracts and for purposes not allowed by the Contracts.[93]

While admitting that the approach is novel, the court still concluded that it was not plain and obvious that this cause of action would fail.[94] Therefore, a company or organisation failing to adhere to the AIC triad could form the basis for a valid claim, since being unable to access or count on data should not constitute an ordinary annoyance.

4 Conclusion

By limiting security breach notification laws to a privacy issue, legislators have willingly or unwittingly chosen to narrow the scope of security claims and, therefore, the chances of success of class action suits based on said claims. While the ideal scenario would see privacy breach notification dispositions be conceived more broadly as dealing with security breaches and taken out of privacy legislation to be included into broader texts such as the CCQ or the Information Technology Act, dealing in fantasy lawmaking scenarios remains counterproductive and unhelpful for those individuals who suffer damages following the hundreds of security breaches registered each year.[95]

The idea is therefore not to dismiss privacy concerns as a cause for class action suits, but rather to explore how the other elements of the AIC triad, i.e. the availability and integrity of data – all data, not just private information – can be used to strengthen legal arguments and cases.

With the constant increase in the number of private and public institutions (including the courts)[96] choosing to move towards digital files, the need for strong security measures and policies is unequivocal. While privacy violations continue to sit atop of the list of "bad things that can happen to data", one shouldn't neglect the fact that said list is much longer and needs to be mastered by those who collect data and those whose role it is to ensure that the rights of the data subjects and/or owners are protected.

---

93 *Ibid.* In the same vein, see *Tucci v Peoples Trust Company*, 2017 BCSC 1525.

94 *Ibid* at para 51.

95 See Gemalto, "Breach Level Index" (2018), online: <breachlevelindex.com/>.

96 Ministère de la Justice, "A Plan to Modernise the Justice System" (March 2018), online (pdf): *Ministère de la Justice* <justice.gouv.qc.ca/fileadmin/user_upload/contenu/documents/ En__Anglais_/centredoc/publications/ministere/dossiers/Justice_1819.pdf>.

6 *Cy près* settlements in privacy class actions

Thomas E. Kadri and Ignacio N. Cofone

1 Introduction

In this chapter, we explore *cy près* settlements – a procedural tool that could address some of the challenges raised by privacy class actions. As francophone readers might have guessed, the idea of a *cy près* settlement comes from the ancient French expression "*cy près comme possible*," meaning "as close as possible."[1] *Cy près* is an equitable doctrine with origins in the law of trusts and estates. As far back as the Roman times, the principle developed that, if a testator's will could not be achieved, courts should try to approximate the intention as much as possible rather than defeating it altogether.[2] If, for example, a testator left money to a Montreal-based homeless shelter and no such place existed, a judge might order that the money go toward establishing such a shelter or funding one in a nearby city.

In the class-action context, the *cy près* doctrine allows courts to indirectly benefit class members by distributing settlement funds to the "next best" beneficiary, usually a charity or non-profit organization involved in work "reasonably approximating the interests pursued by the class."[3] Courts have sometimes used this mechanism to disburse unclaimed settlement funds,

---

1 Martin H Redish et al, "Cy Pres Relief and the Pathologies of the Modern Class Action: A Normative and Empirical Analysis" (2010) 62 Fla L Rev 617 at 624.
2 Abraham L Pomerantz, "New Developments in Class Actions – Has Their Death Knell Been Sounded" (1969) 25:3 Bus Lawyer 1259 at 1262; Gail Hillebrand & Daniel Torrence, "Claims Procedures in Large Consumer Class Actions and Equitable Distribution of Benefits" (1988) 28 Santa Clara L Rev 747 at 762–63.
3 *In re Baby Product Antitrust Litigation*, 708 F (3d) 163 at 169 (3d Cir 2013) [*Baby Product Antitrust*]. The first suggestion of using the *cy près* mechanism in class actions appears to be a 1972 student paper. See Stewart R Shepherd, "Comment, Damage Distribution in Class Actions: The Cy Pres Remedy" (1972) 39 U Chicago L Rev 448 at 448. The earliest judicial use, meanwhile, appears to have come two years later in the Southern District of New York's decision in *Miller v Steinbach et al*, 1974 WL 350 at *2 (SD NY Dist Ct 1974).

such as when "class members cannot be located, decline to file claims, have died, or the parties have overestimated the amount projected for distribution."[4]

But another use has begun to gain traction and generate controversy. When courts conclude that it is either too burdensome to prove individual claims or too costly to distribute damages, a *cy près* settlement can give class members some advantage even if they receive no money themselves.[5] One can imagine how this situation might often arise in the context of widespread privacy invasions, where proving any particular individual's harm is often a difficult and expensive task. Instead of letting the defendant walk away scot-free, a court could approve a *cy près* settlement to indirectly benefit class members by funding initiatives to address or prevent similar privacy invasions in the future.

There is a synergy between class actions and the idea of *cy près*. Class actions seek to "collectivize individual claims into a single proceeding, with the overwhelming majority of the plaintiffs assuming a purely passive role in the proceeding."[6] In so doing, class actions aim to resolve claims that are too numerous to litigate individually. The types of claims raised in class actions are often worth little on an individual basis. Indeed, this feature is precisely what makes class actions an appealing procedural tool; the cost for any particular plaintiff to litigate their claim would exceed the meager payout they could receive even if they are successful. By consolidating hundreds – sometimes thousands – of individual claims, class actions enable courts to adjudicate allegations of serious and widespread harm. Nevertheless, when successful claims are worth so little, the costs of notifying class members and dispersing settlement funds to thousands of claimants can consume a sizeable portion of the claim's value and sometimes even exceed it. In these circumstances, the *cy près* mechanism can serve the law's deterrent effect, saving class actions that might otherwise be economically or practically unfeasible.

Class actions face two additional administrability problems that bear on the *cy près* mechanism. First, in many jurisdictions, class actions function

4 *In re: Google Inc Cookie Placement Consumer Privacy Litigation*, 934 F (3d) 316 at 326–27 (3d Cir 2019) [*Google Cookie*] (quoting *Baby Product Antitrust, supra* note 3 at 169); see also Cecily C Shiel, "A New Generation of Class Action Cy Pres Remedies: Lessons from Washington State Notes & Comments" (2015) 90 Wash L Rev 943 at 945.

5 Indirect compensation paid to an organization, in lieu of compensation to members who cannot be compensated directly, is sometimes referred to as a "residual amount." See *Option Consommateurs c Banque Nationale du Canada*, 2015 QCCS 4380 [*Option Consommateurs v BNC*].

6 Redish et al, *supra* note 1 at 618.

as "opt-out" regimes: class members do not affirmatively choose to be part of the class and must opt out if they are displeased with the settlement and wish to pursue individual claims.[7] Although courts attempt to notify class members of their legal rights, many people likely become part of class actions without being fully aware of it. Second, in order to make their work worthwhile, class counsel will generally get a sizeable fee for their services as part of any settlement[8] – a fee that usually dwarfs the per-person award of each class member. Taken together, these common characteristics in class actions can enable abuse unless closely monitored by the supervising judges. As we explain below, this is particularly true when *cy près* settlements are involved.

This chapter addresses the difficult question, also explored in the preceding chapters of this book, of how to redress the harm to plaintiffs who experience privacy invasions. More directly, this chapter explores the particular mechanism of *cy près* settlements, which, while not without its risks and faults, can help to deter privacy invasions, enforce privacy laws, and provide plaintiffs with some measure of relief when those laws are violated. Despite the controversy surrounding *cy près* settlements, with proper judicial supervision, they can be an especially useful tool in privacy class actions.

2 *Cy près* in *Frank v. Gaos*

The recent U.S. Supreme Court case *Frank v. Gaos* reveals how *cy près* settlements can help in privacy class actions while also illuminating how they might be abused.

As every reader will know, when a user types something into Google's search engine, it displays links to all sorts of websites. Less well known is that, when the user clicks on one of those links, Google tells the website operator what search terms led the user to that page. For example, if someone searches for "Law Schools in Canada" and then clicks on a link to McGill's website, McGill will know that those search terms were used to arrive at its website.

Objecting to this practice, a group of plaintiffs in *Frank v. Gaos* filed a class action against Google in California claiming that the company had violated their privacy rights by disclosing their search terms to operators

7 Catherine Piché & Genevieve Saumier, "Consumer Collective Redress in Canada" (2018) 61 Japanese YB Intl L 231 at 240.
8 Janet Walker et al, *Class Actions in Canada: Cases, Notes, and Materials*, 2nd ed (Toronto: Emond Publishing, 2018) at 218.

of other websites.[9] The plaintiffs alleged that the practice ran afoul of the
Stored Communications Act, an American federal law prohibiting any
entity that provides an "electronic communication service" from "know-
ingly divulg[ing] . . . the contents of a communication" stored by that service.[10] The act also creates a private right of action entitling any "person
aggrieved by any violation" to recover "appropriate" relief from whatever
entity "engaged in that violation."[11]

The plaintiffs reached a settlement with Google under which Google
would pay $8.5 million. Although Google was not required to cease the
practice of sharing search terms with third parties, the company pledged
in the settlement to provide information on its website about how it shares
search terms outside of Google.[12] In exchange for this settlement, the
approximately 129 million people who had used Google's search engine in
recent years would have their claims extinguished.[13]

Even for a company of Google's size, an $8.5 million settlement might
appear significant for this kind of privacy invasion. But the size of the class
meant that no particular plaintiff would feel wealthy after cashing their settlement cheque. In fact, when all was said and done, the settlement would
have amounted to roughly four cents per person. Faced with this puny per-
person award, the district court accepted the parties' argument that the cost
of verifying each claim and dispersing minuscule payments to millions of
class members "would exceed the total monetary benefit obtained by the
class."[14]

It was at this point that the *cy près* mechanism became quite appealing.
Instead of making millions of class members a few cents richer, why not
pool their money and put it toward something that might better serve the
privacy interests animating the case? This was the path taken in the *Frank*
case, in which the court and the parties' lawyers agreed that it would be
better to give the money to privacy-focused non-profits to advance privacy
interests in the future. From the $8.5 million settlement, around $3 million would go toward attorneys' fees, administration costs, and incentive
payments to the named plaintiffs. The remaining $5 million would go to

9 *Frank v Gaos*, 139 S Ct 1041 at 1044 (2019) [*Frank*]. One of the chapter authors, Thomas
Kadri, briefly worked as a law clerk on the *Frank v Gaos* case, but the perspectives shared
here are based only on public documents.
10 *Ibid.*
11 *Ibid.*
12 *In re Google Referrer Header Privacy Litigation*, 869 F (3d) 737 at 740 (9th Cir 2017)
[*Google Referrer*], vacated and remanded sub nom *Frank, supra* note 9.
13 *Ibid.*
14 *Ibid* at 742.

six non-profits that agreed to use the money to promote awareness, education, and research on "protecting privacy on the Internet."[15] These *cy près* recipients included prominent organizations in the privacy and tech space, including Harvard's Berkman Klein Center, Stanford's Center for Internet and Society, and the World Privacy Forum.

In a class of 129 million people, 13 people opted out of the settlement and 5 objected. The objectors argued that it was impermissible to award only *cy près* relief without giving the class members any monetary benefit – a so-called "*cy près*–only settlement." They also alleged that conflicts of interest "infected" the selection of these *cy près* recipients.[16] But after considering these complaints, the district court approved the settlement as "fair, reasonable, and adequate" under Federal Rule of Civil Procedure 23, which governs class actions in the United States.[17]

When the Court of Appeals reviewed the *Frank* case, it held that the district court did not abuse its discretion by approving the *cy près*–only settlement.[18] Although the appellate court noted the district court's complaint that some of the non-profits were the "usual suspects" to receive these kinds of awards and that some of the organizations were based at law schools where the plaintiffs' lawyers had obtained their law degrees, the appellate court concluded that nothing in the record "raise[d] substantial questions" about whether the selections were made "on the merits."[19]

The objectors decided to take their case to the Supreme Court of the United States, likely buoyed by the fact that at least one influential member of the Supreme Court seemed skeptical about the propriety of *cy près* settlements. When a similar case was appealed to the court in 2013, the justices declined to hear it, but Chief Justice John Roberts wrote a separate statement that invited litigants to bring appropriate cases "to clarify the limits on the use of [*cy près*] remedies."[20] Among the chief justice's "fundamental concerns" were whether courts should ever use the *cy près* mechanism, how courts should assess the "fairness" of *cy près* settlements, how non-profit recipients should be selected, and "how closely the goals of any enlisted organization must correspond to the interests of the class."[21]

---

15 *Ibid* at 740.
16 *Frank, supra* note 9 at 1045.
17 *Google Referrer, supra* note 12 at 742–43.
18 *Ibid* at 743, 747.
19 *Ibid* at 743–44, 746–47.
20 *Marek v Lane*, 571 US 1003 at 9 (2013) (Roberts, CJ, statement respecting denial of *certiorari*).
21 *Ibid*.

In *Frank v. Gaos*, it seemed that we were destined to get answers to some of these questions. The Supreme Court agreed to hear the case to decide whether a *cy près*–only settlement can ever be "fair, reasonable, and adequate" under Rule 23.[22] There was anticipation that the Supreme Court's decision could have broad implications for the way that money would be distributed in class actions.[23] But after the government filed a brief questioning the plaintiffs' standing to bring their claims, the court dodged the *cy près* question and remanded the case to the lower courts to determine whether the plaintiffs had standing in light of the court's 2016 decision in *Spokeo, Inc. v. Robins*, an important case about standing to bring privacy claims.[24]

Although the court did not pass judgment on the propriety of *cy près* settlements, we can now be confident that at least one other justice believes that they are problematic. In a dissent from the *Frank* decision, Justice Clarence Thomas asserted that the *cy près* settlement was impermissible because the class members received "no settlement fund, no meaningful injunctive relief, and no other benefit whatsoever in exchange for the settlement of their claims."[25] If objectors to *cy près* settlements return to the court, they will likely find an ally in Justice Thomas.

The case law surrounding *cy près* settlements leaves many unanswered questions. Can a *cy près*–only settlement ever be "fair, reasonable, and adequate" under Rule 23? How do *cy près*–only settlements relate to Rule 23's "superiority" requirement, under which the court must conclude that the class action mechanism is "superior" to adjudicating claims on an individual basis? How much should one worry about conflicts of interest in this area? What kind of oversight should courts provide to determine which *cy près* recipients are appropriate? Does the *cy près* doctrine raise constitutional concerns by offending separation of powers?[26]

---

22 Kevin M Lewis, "UPDATE: Is Cy Pres A-OK? Supreme Court to Consider When Class Action Settlements Can Pay a Charity Instead of Class Members" (2019) at 3, online (pdf): *Congressional Research Service* <fas.org/sgp/crs/misc/LSB10131.pdf>.

23 *Ibid* at 4.

24 See *Spokeo, Inc v Robins*, 136 S Ct 1540 (2016).

25 *Frank, supra* note 9 at 1048 (Thomas, J, dissenting).

26 See Redish et al, *supra* note 1 at 622–23 (arguing that *cy près* "contravenes the adversary 'bilateralism' constitutionally required by the adjudicatory process embodied in Article III's case-or-controversy requirement"); Omri Ben-Shahar & Ariel Porat, "The Restoration Remedy in Private Law" (2018) 118 Colum L Rev 1901 at 1937 (observing that "[c]y pres raises fundamental questions about the authority of courts to select nonlitigants as the recipients of court-awarded damages"); *Klier v Elf Atochem North America, Inc*, 658 F (3d) 468 at 480–82 (5th Cir 2011) [*Klier*] (Jones, CJ, concurring) (expressing concern that *cy près* distributions may violate Article III standing requirements).

Although answering all of these questions is beyond the scope of this chapter, we offer some thoughts on how *cy près* settlements can be particularly helpful in the context of privacy class actions and how courts can mitigate some concerns about abuse in this area.

3 The particular usefulness of *cy près* for privacy class actions

Cy près settlements are particularly useful when compensating victims is impracticable or impossible.[27] In these circumstances, the *cy près* mechanism allows courts to instead apportion settlement funds in ways that indirectly benefit class members and serve the "societal goals" underlying privacy laws.[28]

While all class actions seek to address the issue of having large numbers of plaintiffs with relatively small claims, privacy class actions often suffer a particularly dire strand of this problem. The difference is primarily in degree, not in kind: compared to other claims frequently brought in class actions, privacy harms are often suffered by larger groups and are often harder to determine,[29] leading to lower individual amounts of compensable harm.

Consider the 2017 Equifax data breach, in which 147 million taxpayers' financial information fell into the hands of unknown recipients.[30] This

---

27 See Ben-Shahar & Porat, *supra* note 26 at 1935 (noting that "[c]lass action recovery often faces the practical problem of identifying the class members and distributing damages to them, especially when the harm to each member of the class is small"); Peter C Ormerod, "A Private Enforcement Remedy for Information Misuse" (2019) 60:7 Boston College L Rev 1893 at 1918 (observing that "[s]ometimes courts order *cy pres* settlements in class actions when it's impracticable to distribute a reward or settlement to the class"); *Lane v Facebook, Inc*, 696 F (3d) 811 at 825 (9th Cir 2012) (concluding that "it would be 'burdensome' and inefficient to pay the . . . funds that remain after costs directly to the class because each class member's recovery under a direct distribution would be *de minimis*" (quoting *Molski v Gleich*, 318 F (3d) 937 at 955 (9th Cir 2003))); *Klier, supra* note 26 at 475 no 15 ("In large class actions, substantial administrative costs attend the distribution of settlement funds. As the settlement funds are disbursed and the amount still available for distribution . . . declines, . . . the marginal cost of making an additional pro rata distribution to the class members exceeds the amount available for distribution.").

28 See Ben-Shahar & Porat, *supra* note 26 at 1935–36; see also Pomerantz, *supra* note 2 at 1260–61; *Berry v LexisNexis Risk & Information Analytics Group, Inc*, 2014 WL 4403524 at *7 (ED Va Dist Ct 2014), aff'd sub nom *Berry v Schulman*, 807 F (3d) 600 (4th Cir 2015); *In re Netflix Privacy Litigation*, 2013 WL 1120801 at *2 (ND Cal Dist Ct 2013); *In re Google Buzz Privacy Litigation*, 2011 WL 7460099 at *4 (ND Cal Dist Ct 2011).

29 Ignacio N Cofone & Adriana Z Robertson, "Privacy Harms" (2018) 69 Hastings LJ 1039; Ignacio N Cofone, "Nothing to Hide, but Something to Lose" (2019) 70:1 UTLJ 64.

30 *Equifax Data Breach Settlement*, Federal Trade Commission (January 2020), online: <www.ftc.gov/enforcement/cases-proceedings/refunds/equifax-data-breach-settlement>.

breach caused privacy harms to millions of people, as well as an indiscernible amount of financial harm (largely to accrue in the future) to an unknown subset of those people. In a settlement with the Federal Trade Commission and the Consumer Financial Protection Bureau, the company agreed to pay $425 million, which works out to less than $3 per victim. The hassle and expense of finding and paying all of these victims would likely exceed any benefit – monetary or otherwise – that would come from giving each person a share of the settlement. The Equifax case was an enforcement action, not a class action, and it did not result in a *cy près* settlement. But the nature of the Equifax data breach provides a compelling example to illustrate the potential benefits of *cy près* in privacy class actions.

In circumstances like those created by the Equifax data breach, *cy près* settlements can offer a way to distribute settlement funds that would otherwise be non-distributable.[31] Even if the funds could feasibly be distributed, the *cy près* mechanism could still better serve class members' interests in cases where each individual payment would be miniscule.[32] In the Equifax case, for example, each individual can do little with $3 – and even less with whatever remains once administration and postage fees are deducted. In other words, notice and distribution costs leave injured persons with little or nothing. But $425 million from Equifax could substantially benefit consumers if invested in organizations that work diligently to protect consumers' privacy and security interests. While the non-distribution problem might occur infrequently in consumer law, it is the norm in privacy law. And while it might be harder to find appropriate organizations to indirectly benefit the class in other doctrinal areas, there are plenty of worthy candidates when privacy interests are involved.

Importantly, by resolving the logistical issue of dispersing settlement funds that would otherwise be economically or practically unfeasible to distribute, the *cy près* mechanism serves valuable policy objectives underlying privacy class actions. Absent a way to distribute these funds, privacy laws might be enforced less regularly. By making more privacy class actions viable, *cy prés* settlements preserve the deterrent effect of privacy laws even when the per-person damages awarded are small or the harm is difficult to ascertain. At a time where many people rightly believe we need greater enforcement of privacy laws, this represents a significant benefit that *cy près* settlements can secure.

As was observed by the law student who, 40 years ago, initially proposed using the *cy près* mechanism in class actions, courts could use *cy près* awards

---

31 Michael J Slobom, "Recalibrating Cy Pres Settlements to Restore the Equilibrium" (2018) 123 Dick L Rev 281 at 306.

32 Lewis, *supra* note 22 at 2.

to navigate the "distribution problems" that arise in some class actions and allocate settlement funds in other ways "designed to maximize public benefit."[33] At the very least, it is worth exploring alternative compensation schemes in tort law, especially schemes that could address systemic issues more effectively.[34] The *cy près* mechanism deserves serious consideration on this ground, especially in the face of the many privacy concerns brought about by the digital age.

4 The challenges of implementing *cy près*

Notwithstanding the usefulness of *cy près* settlements for privacy law, they do raise some concerns. *Cy près* settlements have triggered skepticism in courts,[35] scholarship,[36] and the media.[37] As Judge Richard Posner once wrote when reviewing the propriety of a particular *cy près* settlement:

> Would it be too cynical to speculate that what may be going on here is that class counsel wanted a settlement that would give them a gener-ous fee and [the defendant] wanted a settlement that would extinguish 1.4 million claims against it at no cost to itself? The settlement that the district judge approved sold these 1.4 million claimants down the river. Only if they had no claim – more precisely no claim large enough to justify a distribution to them – did they lose nothing by the settlement, and the judge made no finding that they had no such claim.[38]

Some scholars have recommended modifying the legal standards governing *cy près* settlements or prohibiting them entirely.[39] A prominent criticism

33 Shepherd, *supra* note 3 at 457.
34 Daniel Jutras, "Alternative Compensation Schemes from a Comparative Perspective" in Mauro Bussani & Anthony J Sebok, eds, *Comparative Tort Law: Global Perspectives* (Cheltenham, UK: Edward Elgar Publishing, 2015) 151.
35 See e.g. *Klier, supra* note 26 at 480–81; *SEC v Bear, Stearns & Co, Inc*, 626 F Supp (2d) 402 (SD NY Dist Ct 2009); *In re Pharmaceutical Industry Average Wholesale Price Litigation*, 588 F (3d) 24 at 34 (1st Cir 2009).
36 See e.g. Sam Yospe, "Cy Pres Distributions in Class Action Settlements" (2009) 2009:3 Colum Bus L Rev 1014 at 1027–41; Goutam U Jois, "The Cy Pres Problem and the Role of Damages in Tort Law" (2008) 16 Va J Soc Policy & L 258 at 259; John Goodlander, "Cy Pres Settlements: Problems Associated with the Judiciary's Role and Suggested Solutions" (2015) 56:2 Boston College L Rev 733 at 735.
37 See Adam Liptak, "Doling Out Other People's Money" (November 26, 2007), online: *The New York Times* <www.nytimes.com/2007/11/26/washington/26bar.html>; George G Krueger & Judd A Serotta, "Money for Nothing" (June 2, 2008) *Legal Times*.
38 *Mirfasihi v Fleet Mortg Corp*, 356 F (3d) 781 at 785 (7th Cir 2004).
39 Lewis, *supra* note 22 at 3.

is that the *cy près* mechanism creates improper incentives to settle cases by exacerbating a pre-existing conflict of interest in many class actions.[40] Class action lawyers generally have an agency problem because they have larger incentives than class members to settle claims instead of litigating them. The lawyers' legal fees for litigating class actions come from settlement funds or final judgments, and the lawyers must cover the costs of investigating and litigating the claims for as long as the class action is alive. Thus, if class action lawyers settle the case, they get paid sooner and can begin litigating other cases; if they fail to settle, they face the full costs of litigation.[41] *Cy près* settlements might aggravate this agency problem: the path to settlement is easier if the lawyers can also avoid navigating difficult distribution issues.[42]

A second critique is that the recipients of *cy près* funds are sometimes poorly chosen, such as when awards go to organizations with only tenuous connections to the class members' interests.[43] Consider the settlement in a 2005 antitrust case about advertising prices for CDs in which the court approved a *cy près* award to an organization that promotes community art projects.[44] As one analysis of this case concluded, "[t]here was no way that the designation even arguably compensated injured victims, directly or indirectly, in any recognizable way."[45] In another controversial case, a court approved a *cy près* award to the American Red Cross Disaster Relief Fund in a class action about infant formula.[46] At times, it appears that the award decisions are especially arbitrary, like when a court approved a *cy près* award to a legal aid society in a securities fraud lawsuit because the society's work was more closely related to securities fraud than would be "a dance performance or a zoo."[47]

---

40 Asher A Cohen, "Settling Cy Pres Settlements: Analyzing the Use of Cy Pres Class Action Settlements" (2019) 32 Geo J Leg Ethics 451 at 459–62.

41 Jennifer Johnston, "Cy Pres Comme Possible to anything is Possible: How Cy Pres Creates Improper Incentives in Class Action Settlements" (2013) 9 JL Economics & Policy 277.

42 Cohen, *supra* note 40 at 459–62.

43 See Marc Rotenberg & David Jacobs, "Enforcing Privacy Rights: Class Action Litigation and the Challenge of Cy Pres" in David Wright & Paul De Hert, eds, *Enforcing Privacy: Regulatory, Legal and Technological Approaches* (Cham, Switzerland: Springer, 2016) at 307–33; Robert E Draba, "Motorsports Merchandise: A Cy Pres Distribution Not Quite 'as Near as Possible'" (2004) 16:2 Loyola Consumer L Rev 121 at 124; Yospe, *supra* note 36 at 1017.

44 *In re Compact Disc Minimum Advertised Price Antitrust Litigation*, 2005 WL 1923446 (D Me Dist Ct 2005).

45 Redish et al, *supra* note 1 at 637.

46 *In re Infant Formula Multidistrict Litigation*, 2005 WL 2211312 at *1 (ND Fla Dist Ct 2005).

47 *Jones v National Distillers*, 56 F Supp (2d) 355 at 359 para [5] (SD NY Dist Ct 1999).

In light of examples like these, it is no wonder that critics have claimed that some *cy près* awards do not "constitute even a feeble attempt to indirectly compensate victims."[48] The mismatch between the victims' interests and the recipients' work could have many causes, but a particularly concerning situation arises when class counsel's recommendations are infected by a conflict of interest. Worse still would be if a *cy près* recipient had pre-existing connections with the defendants that raise concerns about collusion and the extent to which the recipient will fight against similar privacy invasions in the future. These concerns, though, are not criticisms of the procedural mechanism in itself, but rather a warning of the need for robust judicial oversight in its application.

Even if no actual conflict of interest exists, some worry about the appearance of conflicts. There is concern that the public might look askance at judges approving large *cy près* awards to private organizations. Even if the organizations are non-profits, the public might be troubled by this entanglement between public and private actors.[49] To avoid sullying the judiciary, some scholars have proposed that courts should instead order defendants to pay money to the state treasury when compensating class members is impracticable.[50] Others have argued that the best way to salvage the *cy près* mechanism is to remove judges from the selection process and instead have the parties stipulate to certain beneficiary organizations as part of the settlement.[51] Additionally, at least one judge has suggested that courts should avoid the *cy près* mechanism entirely by returning excess funds to the defendant instead of picking *cy près* recipients.[52] Again, these concerns seem motivated largely by how courts implement the *cy près* mechanism. Particular settlements can certainly invite the public's distrust, but judicial oversight need not mean judicial complicity. Judges should take special care to avoid any appearance of impropriety when approving awards in *cy près* settlements.

5 Implementing *cy près* in a bijural Canada

The application, conception, and characteristics of the *cy près* doctrine vary between civil law and common law systems, and even differ among

---

48 Redish et al, *supra* note 1 at 637.
49 See Chris Trivisonno, "Developing a Consistent Approach to Balance Distributions in Quebec" (2016) 11 Can Class Action Rev 321 at 338; *Sorenson v Easyhome Ltd*, 2013 ONSC 4017.
50 See e.g. Ormerod, *supra* note 27 at 1948.
51 See Goodlander, *supra* note 36 at 736–37.
52 See *Klier, supra* note 26 at 480–82 (Jones, CJ, concurring).

jurisdictions within the same system. As an initial matter, class actions in most common law systems, including the United States, have an opt-out process, in which injured persons are automatically included in the class and then may opt out later if they wish.[53] In civil law systems, by contrast, courts must generally determine injured persons and certainty of the harm in advance, and accordingly injured persons must affirmatively join a class before they are eligible for compensation.[54] The result is that injured persons must join a class in advance to receive compensation in civil law systems, whereas they may justify their class membership after courts decide to compensate the class in common law systems like the United States.[55]

Perhaps due to this distinction, judges in some civil law systems have fashioned a slightly different use of the *cy près* mechanism: to benefit individuals who have not opted into the class. This application of *cy près* exists in some Latin American countries, particularly Brazil, Mexico, and Chile.[56] Recall that the *cy près* mechanism in common law systems is residual, meaning that it should be used only when class members cannot be compensated directly.[57] In other words, "[i]ndirect compensation paid to an organization, in lieu of compensation to members who cannot be compensated directly" is the exception and not the rule.[58] This presumption in favour of direct compensation appears to be weaker in some Latin American counties. In Brazil, courts have wide discretionary power to decide on appropriate redress,[59] while the residual characteristic of *cy près* is absent in Mexico and Chile, where the legal frameworks establish beforehand the destination of unclaimed amounts.[60] This has led some commentators to consider that these Latin American versions of *cy près* settlements, by focusing on deterrence at the expense of compensation even when compensation is possible, may contradict the idea of "as close as possible" set forth by common law systems.[61]

These distinctions between some common and civil law systems could lead one to believe that the scope of *cy près* settlements in Canada would differ between Quebec and common law provinces. However, the Code

53 Javier Esteban Rodríguez Diez & María Elisa Zavala Achurra, "Restitución e Indemnización a Sujetos Indeterminados, Cy-Près y Acciones de Clase" (2019) 21 Estudios Socio-Jurídicos 151 at 154.
54 *Ibid* at 166–67.
55 *Ibid* at 162, 166–67.
56 *Ibid* at 168–73.
57 *Ibid* at 158, 171.
58 See *Option Consommateurs v BNC, supra* note 5.
59 Rodríguez Diez & Zavala Achurra, *supra* note 53 at 168.
60 *Ibid* at 169–70.
61 *Ibid* at 170, 172.

of Civil Procedure in Quebec contemplates *cy près* awards,[62] and Quebec case law has remained close to that of Canadian common law provinces where *cy près* awards have been approved.[63] The *cy près* doctrine in Quebec is also residual.[64] Indeed, *cy près* distributions are not unheard of in Quebec, though they are sometimes mistakenly perceived as uncommon because many are unreported.[65] At a broad level, Quebec's embrace of *cy près* could be seen as an illustration of how the common law influences civil law in Quebec (and vice versa), in what has been called a "cross-fertilization" of Canada's two legal traditions.[66]

In Canada, it is uncontroversial that class actions serve dual purposes of behavioural modification and deterrence, on the one hand, and compensation, on the other.[67] But opinions differ as to the weight due to each of these purposes. Some have argued that Canadian judges have generally shown a preference for the compensatory function of civil litigation over the deterrence function,[68] while many have cast doubt on the assertion that class actions in general are effective at compensating citizens.[69] Accordingly, although a number of Canadian provinces have authorized *cy près* in provincial class action statutes, this move has not been without controversy.[70] Nevertheless, courts have begun to use the *cy près* mechanism in multiple Canadian provinces. In a 2018 case, for example, a court in British Columbia distributed damages to local schools after they remained unclaimed for

---

62 See Arts 590, 593, 596, 597 CCP. Before the new code came into effect in 2015, *cy près* settlements were contemplated in Arts 1033, 1034, 1036 CCP (1965).

63 See e.g. *D'Urzo v Tnow Entertainment Group*, 2014 QCCS 365 (following Ontario's strict approach to the rational connection between the interests of the members and the one or more beneficiaries to whom the settlement fund is to be distributed); see also *MD c Hôpital Rivière-des-Prairies*, 2016 QCCS 2651; *Adams v Banque Amex du Canada*, 2015 QCCS 1917; *Option consommateurs v Infineon Technologies*, 2019 QCCA 2132 at paras 64–68.

64 See *Handicap-Vie-Dignité c Résidence St-Charles-Borromée, CHSLD Centre-ville de Montréal*, 2017 QCCS 935; *Option Consommateurs v BNC*, *supra* note 5.

65 Jasminka Kalajdzic, "The 'Illusion of Compensation': Cy Pres Distributions in Canadian Class Actions" (2013) 92:2 Can Bar Rev 173 n 62.

66 Rosalie Jukier, "Canada's Legal Traditions: Sources of Unification, Diversification, or Inspiration?" (2018) 11 J Civ L Studies 75; Rosalie Jukier, "The Impact of Legal Traditions on Quebec Procedural Law: Lessons from Quebec's New Code of Civil Procedure" (2015) 93 Can Bar Rev 211; Daniel Jutras, "Cartographie de la Mixité: La Common Law et la Complétude du Droit Civil au Québec" (2009) 88 La Revue du Barreau Canadien 247.

67 Jeff Berryman & Robyn Carroll, "Cy-Pres as a Class Action Remedy – Justly Maligned or Just Misunderstood?" in Kit Barker & Darryn Jensen, eds, *Private Law: Key Encounters with Public Law* (Cambridge: Cambridge University Press, 2013) at 320–65.

68 Kalajdzic, *supra* note 65.

69 Catherine Piché, "Class Action Value" (2018) 19:1 Theoretical Inquiries in L 261.

70 Kalajdzic, *supra* note 65 at 191–93.

ten months,[71] and another court in Ontario authorized a *cy près* award to a charity in a 2019 case after plaintiffs attempted to discontinue the action.[72] The considerations set out in this chapter suggest that, as privacy class actions continue to grow in popularity in Canada, judges in provinces that authorize *cy près* settlements should give them special consideration in cases involving privacy claims.

In sum, *cy près* settlements can be a valuable tool for privacy class actions in Canada because courts in both Quebec and common law provinces have embraced this type of settlement distribution. While some Canadian courts have shared the skepticism shown by some courts in the United States, Canadian law has set the stage to welcome the benefits of *cy près* settlements in privacy class actions.

6 Conclusion

Cy près settlements reignite an old discussion about the purposes of civil lawsuits: restitution and deterrence. Some civil remedies serve both purposes in harmony, while others favour one over the other. *Cy près* settlements underperform in restitution because they have "no ambition to cure the harm suffered by the specific plaintiffs" and instead seek "to bolster a set of values and interests related to that harm."[73] To be sure, if allocated appropriately, class members should receive *indirect* benefits when organizations receive *cy près* awards, thereby helping the mechanism align with remedial goals. But even if done properly, these indirect benefits do not constitute compensation to make class members whole, and there is no post-hoc judicial supervision to ensure that any intended indirect benefits materialize.

An important justification for *cy près* settlements, then, lies in their ability to offer some deterrence of unlawful behaviour. While *cy près* settlements serve the goal of restitution only tangentially, they can deter unlawful behaviour more effectively than returning non-distributable settlement funds to the defendant.[74] Moreover, the *cy près* mechanism "more closely tailors the distribution to the interests of class members" than simply escheating non-distributable funds to the state.[75] The potential for abuse makes it especially important that *cy près* funds are disbursed to entities closely related to the cause of action, but this can be ensured by robust scrutiny by courts. With adequate judicial supervision, *cy près* settlements can be a valuable tool in privacy class actions. Courts should not give up on them quite yet.

71 *Pro-Sys Consultants Ltd v Microsoft Corporation*, 2018 BCSC 2091.
72 *Ali Holdco Inc v Archer Daniels Midland Company*, 2019 ONSC 131.
73 Ben-Shahar & Porat, *supra* note 26 at 1937.
74 See Lewis, *supra* note 22 at 2; see also *Google Cookie*, *supra* note 4.
75 *Ibid.*

Bibliography

Legislation

Act respecting Access to documents held by public bodies and the Protection of personal information, CQLR c A-2.1.

Act respecting the Protection of Personal Information in the Private Sector, RSQ, c. P-39.1.

Act respecting the protection of personal information in the private sector, CQLR c P-39.1.

Act to establish a legal framework for information technology, CQLR c C-1.1 (English and French versions).

Arthur Wishart Act (Franchise Disclosure), 2000, SO 2002, c 3.

Biometric Information Privacy Act, 740 Ill Comp Stat 14/1.

Breach of Security Safeguards Regulations, SOR/2018-64.

British Columbia Court Jurisdiction and Proceedings Transfer Act.

Business Practices and Consumer Protection Act, SBC 2004, c 2.

California Consumer Privacy Act of 2018, Cal Civ Code tit 1.81.5

Charter of Human Rights and Freedoms, CQLR c C-12.

Civil Code of Québec, CQLR c CCQ-1991.

Class Proceedings Act, 1992, SO 1992, c 6.

Code of Civil Procedure, CQLR c C-25.01.

Code of Civil Procedure, CQLR c C-25.

Communications Decency Act, 47 USC § 230.

Consumer Protection Act, CCSM c C200.

Criminal Code, RSC 1985, c C-46.

Digital Privacy Act, SC 2015, c 32.

Divorce Act, RSC 1985, c 3 (2nd Supp).

EC, *Regulation (EU) 2016/679 of 27 April 2016 on the protection of natural persons with regard to the processing of personal data and on the free movement of such data, and repealing Directive 95/46/ EC (General Data Protection Regulation)*, [2016] OJ, L 119.

EC, *Regulation (EU) No 1215/2012 of 12 December 2012 on jurisdiction and the recognition and enforcement of judgments in civil and commercial matters*.

EC, *Regulation (EC) No 593/2008 on the law applicable to contractual obligations*.

Family Law Act, RSO 1990, c F.3.

Health Information Privacy and Management Act, SY 2013, c 16.

International Choice of Court Agreements Convention Act, 2017 SO 2017, c 2, Sch 4.

Marine Liability Act, SC 2001, c 6.

OECD, *Guidelines on the Protection of Privacy and Transborder Flows of Personal Data* (1980).

Personal Health Information Protection Act, 2004, SO 2004, c 3, Sch A.

Personal Information Protection Act, SBC 2003, c 63.

Personal Information Protection Act, SA 2003, c P-6.5.

Personal Information Protection and Electronic Documents Act, SC 2000, c 5.

Privacy Act, RSBC 1996, c 373.

Privacy Act, RSC 1985, c P-21.

Privacy Act, RSN 1990, c P-22.

Privacy Act, RSM 1987 c P-125.

Privacy Act, RSS 1978, c P-24.

Public Health Act, CQLR c S-2.2.

Restatement (Second) of Torts § 652D (1976).

Jurisprudence

Adams v Banque Amex du Canada, 2015 QCCS 1917.

Albilia v Apple Inc, 2014 QCCS 5311.

Albilia v Apple Inc, 2013 QCCS 2805.

Agnew-Americano v Equifax Canada Co, 2018 ONSC 275.

AIC Limited v Fischer, 2013 SCC 69.

Aldo Group Inc v Moneris Solutions Corporation, 2013 ONCA 725.

Ali Holdco Inc v Archer Daniels Midland Company, 2019 ONSC 131.

Amchem Products Inc v British Columbia (Workers' Compensation Board), [1993] 1 SCR 897, 102 DLR (4th) 96.

Antman v Uber Technologies, Inc, 2018 WL 2151231 (ND Cal 2018).

Ari v Insurance Corporation of British Columbia, 2015 BCCA 468.

A.T. v Globe24h.com, 2017 FC 114.

AT&T Mobility LLC v Concepcion, 563 US 333 (2011).

Austin v Bell Canada, 2018 ONSC 4018.

Azam v Equifax Inc and Equifax Canada Co, ONSC, filed on September 18, 2017.

Ballantine v Equifax Inc, and Equifax Canada Co, ONSC File No CV-17-582566.

Banadyga v Wal-Mart Canada Corp, 2016 SKQB 405.

Belley v TD Auto Finance Services Inc, 2015 QCCS 168.

Bennett v Lenovo (Canada), 2017 ONSC 5853.

Bergeron c Banque Royale du Canada, 2006 QCCS 5226.

Berry v LexisNexis Risk & Information Analytics Group, Inc, 2014 WL 4403524 (ED Va Dist Ct 2014).

Berry v Schulman, 807 F (3d) 600 (4th Cir 2015).

Biron v RBC Royal Bank, 2012 FC 1095.

Boardwalk Regency Corp v Maalouf (1992), 6 OR (3d) 737 (CA), [1992] OJ No 26 (QL).

Bourbonnière v Yahoo! Inc, 2019 QCCS 2624.

Broutzas v Rouge Valley Health System, 2018 ONSC 6315.

Bywater v Toronto Transit Commission, 43 OR (3d) 367, [1999] OJ No 1402.

Canada v John Doe, 2016 FCA 191.

Capital District Health Authority v Murray, 2017 NSCA 28.

*Centre Financier aux Entreprises Desjardins Grandes Seigneuries Vallée des Tiss-
erands v Syndicat des Employées et Employés Professionnels et de Bureau, Section Locale 575*, AZ-50507770.

Chadha v Bayer Inc, 223 DLR (4th) 158, OR (3d) 22.

Chamberlain v Facebook, Inc and Facebook Canada Inc, ONSC File No CV-18-
598747OOCP.

Chasles v Bell Canada Inc, 2017 QCCS 5200.

Chu v Parwell Investments Inc et al, 2019 ONSC 700.

Condon v Canada, 2018 FC 522.

Condon v Canada, 2014 FC 250.

Condon v Canada, 2015 FCA 159.

Connelly v RTZ Corporation plc, [1997] UKHL 30, [1998] AC 854.

Cook v Lewis, [1951] SCR 830, [1952] 1 DLR 1.

Daniel Thalheimer v Equifax, BCSC, filed on August 27, 2018.

Daniel Li v Equifax Inc et Equifax Canada Co (September 11, 2017), Montreal, Que
CS, 500-06-000885-174.

Daniells v McLellan, 2017 ONSC 3466.

Dell Computer Corp v Union des consommateurs, 2007 SCC 34.

Demers c Yahoo! Inc, 2017 QCCS 4154.

Doe v The Queen, Fed Ct T-1931-13.

Douez v Facebook, 2018 BCCA 186.

Douez v Facebook, Inc, 2017 SCC 33.

Douez v Facebook, Inc, 2014 BCSC 953.

Drew v Walmart Canada Inc, 2017 ONSC 3308.

Drew v Walmart Canada Inc, 2016 ONSC 8067.

D'Urzo v Tnow Entertainment Group, 2014 QCCS 365.

Elkoby v Google Inc, 2018 QCCS 2623.

Emond and MacQueen v Google LLC, CV-18-590521, 2018.

European Court of Justice C-369/96 and C-376/96 (judgement of the Court of
Justice of 23 November 1999, Jean-Claude Arblade and Arblade & Fils SARL,
C-369/96 and Bernard Leloup, Serge Leloup and Fofrage SARL – C-376/96).

Evans v The Bank of Nova Scotia, 2014 ONSC 2135.

Expedition Helicopters Inc v Honeywell Inc, 2010 ONCA 351.

Fantl v Transamerica Life Canada, [2009] OJ No. 4324, 2009 CanLII 55704 (ONSC).

*Fortier c Uber Canada Inc, Uber Technologies Inc, Uber B.V et Rasier Operations
B.V*, QSC, No: 500-06-000902-185, January 23, 2018.

Frank v Gaos, 139 S Ct 1041 (2019).

Fulawka v Bank of Nova Scotia, 2012 ONCA 443.

Gill v Yahoo! Canada Co, et al, 2018 BCSC 290.

Girao v Zarek Taylor Grossman Hanrahan LLP, 2011 FC 1070.

Google Inc v Equustek Solutions Inc, 2017 SCC 34.

116   *Bibliography*

Google Inc v Equustek Solutions Inc, Case No. 17-CV-04207 (ND Cal Dis Ct).

Hancock v Urban Outfitters, Inc, 830 F (3d) 511 (DC Cir 2016).

Handicap-Vie-Dignité c Résidence St-Charles-Borromée, CHSLD Centre-ville de Montréal, 2017 QCCS 935.

Hemeon v South West Nova District Health Authority, 2015 NSSC 287.

Hollick v Toronto (City), 2001 SCC 68.

Hong Xin Jimmy Mei v Apple Inc et Apple Canada Inc, C.S. Montréal, 500-06-000973-194, filed on January 29, 2019.

Hopkins v Kay, 2015 ONCA 112.

Hryniak v Mauldin, 2014 SCC 7.

Hugo Langlois v Fédération des caisses Desjardins du Québec et als, Montréal 500-06-001009-196, filed on June 21, 2019.

Hynes v Western Regional Integrated Health Authority, 2014 NLTD(G) 137.

In re Baby Product Antitrust Litigation, 708 F (3d) 163 (3d Cir 2013).

In re Compact Disc Minimum Advertised Price Antitrust Litigation, 2005 WL 192 3446 (D Me Dist Ct 2005).

In re Google Buzz Privacy Litigation, 2011 WL 7460099 (ND Cal Dist Ct 2011).

In re Google Inc Cookie Placement Consumer Privacy Litigation, 934 F (3d) 316 (3d Cir 2019).

In re Google Referrer Header Privacy Litigation, 869 F (3d) 737 (9th Cir 2017).

In re Infant Formula Multidistrict Litigation, 2005 WL 2211312 (ND Fla Dist Ct 2005).

In re Netflix Privacy Litigation, 2013 WL 1120801 (ND Cal Dist Ct 2013).

In re Pharmaceutical Industry Average Wholesale Price Litigation, 588 F (3d) 24 (1st Cir 2009).

In re Target Corp Customer Data Sec Breach Litigation, 64 F Supp (3d) 1304 (Minn Dis Ct 2014).

In re TJX Companies, Inc, Customer Data Security Breach Litigation, 493 F Supp (2d) 1382 (Mem) (Judicial Panel on Multidistrict Litigation 2007).

James v Marriott.

Jane Doe 72511 v Morgan, 2018 ONSC 6607.

John Doe v Canada, 2015 FC 916.

Jones v National Distillers, 56 F Supp (2d) 355 (SD NY Dist Ct 1999).

Jones v Tsige, 2012 ONCA 32.

Joshua Elliott Temple v Equifax Inc and Equifax Canada Co, VLC-S-S-180347.

Kaplan v Casino Rama Services Inc, 2017 ONSC 2671.

Karasik v Yahoo! Inc et al, ONSC.

King & Dawson v Government of PEI, 2019 PESC 27.

Klier v Elf Atochem North America, Inc, 658 F (3d) 468 (5th Cir 2011).

Kochar v University of Saskatchewan (1998), [1999] 3 WWR 531, 169 Sask R 119 (SKQB).

Krygier v Marriott, BCSC.

Ladas v Apple Inc, 2014 BCSC 1821.

Lamoureux v Investment Industry Regulatory Organization of Canada (IIROC), 2016 QCCS 4704.

Landry v Royal Bank of Canada, 2011 FC 687.
Lane v Facebook, Inc, 696 F (3d) 811 (9th Cir 2012).
Lavigne v Canada (Office of the Commissioner of Official Languages), 2002 SCC 53.
Leventakis v Facebook, Inc, QSC, 500-06-000938-189, July 20, 2018.
Levy v Nissan Canada Inc, QSC, 500-06-000907-184, February 12, 2018.
Lewert v P.F. Chang's China Bistro, Inc, 819 F (3d) 963 (7th Cir 2016).
Li c Equifax Inc, 2019 QCCS 4340.
Li c Equifax Inc, 2018 QCCS 1892.
Li c Equifax Inc, 200-06-000885-174.
Lima v Google LLC, QSC, 500-06-000940-183 and 500-06-000940-185, August 15, 2018.
L'Oratoire Saint-Joseph du Mont-Royal v J.J., 2019 SCC 35.
Loveseth v Marriott.
Lozanski v Home Depot, Inc, 2016 ONSC 5447.
Lubbe v Cape plc, [2000] UKHL 41.
Lungowe v Vedanta Resources Plc [2019] UKSC 20.
Maksimovic v Sony, 2013 ONSC 4604.
Mallinson v Trillium Health Partners, Dr. A. Tony Vettese and Lisa Lyons, ONSC.
Mann v Marriott, NSSC.
Marek v Lane, 571 US 1003 (2013).
MasterCard International Inc v The Aldo Group Inc et al, 2014 CarswellOnt 5661, 2014 CanLII 21559 (SCC).
Matusevitch v Telnikoff, 877 F Supp 1 (DDC 1995).
Mazzonna v DaimlerChrysler Financial Services Canada Inc, 2012 QCCS 958.
MD c Hôpital Rivière-des-Prairies, 2016 QCCS 2651.
Mei c Apple Inc, 2019 QCCS 4539.
Michael Evans & Crystal Evans v The Bank of Nova Scotia & Richard Wilson, 2014 ONSC 7249.
Michael Forian-Zytynsky & Elisabeth Prass v Capital One Bank & Capital One Financial Corporation, Montreal 500-06-001012-190, filed on July 30, 2019.
Miller v Steinbach et al, 1974 WL 350 (SD NY Dist Ct 1974).
Mirfasihi v Fleet Mortg Corp, 356 F (3d) 781 (7th Cir 2004).
Molski v Gleich, 318 F (3d) 937 955 (9th Cir 2003).
Moran v Pyle National (Canada) Ltd, [1975] 1 SCR 393, 43 DLR (3d) 239.
Morguard Investments Ltd v De Savoye, [1990] 3 SCR 1077, 76 DLR (4th) 256.
Murray v East Coast Forensic Hospital, 2015 NSSC 61.
Mustapha v Culligan of Canada Ltd, 2008 SCC 27.
Old North State Brewing Co, Inc v Newlands Service Inc (1998), 58 BCLR (3d) 144 (CA), [1999] 4 WWR 573.
Option Consommateurs c Banque Nationale du Canada, 2015 QCCS 4380.
Option Consommateurs c Banque Royale, 2009 QCCS 4485.
Option consommateurs v Infineon Technologies, 2019 QCCA 2132.
Plimmer v Google Inc, 2013 BCSC 681.
Pro-Sys Consultants Ltd v Microsoft Corporation, 2018 BCSC 2091.
Ragoonanan v Imperial Tobacco Canada Ltd, 78 OR (3d) 98, [2005] OJ No 4697.

Rechtbank Overijssel [Overijssel District Court], Zwolle, 28 May 2019, AWB 18/2047 (Netherlands) (de Rechtspraak).

Randall v Nubodys Fitness Centres, 2010 FC 681.

Rosenbach v Six Flags Entertainment Corp, 129 NE (3d) 1197 (Ill Sup Ct 2019).

Rowlands v Durham Region Health, et al, 2011 ONSC 719.

Rudder v Microsoft Corp (1999), 40 CPC (4th) 394 (SCJ Ont), 2 CPR (4th) 474.

Rumley v British Columbia, 2001 SCC 69.

Sache v Marriott, BCSC.

Schnarr and Brown v Marriott International Inc, Marriott Hotels of Canada Ltd and Starwood Canada ULC, ONSC.

SEC v Bear, Stearns & Co, Inc, 626 F Supp (2d) 402 (SD NY Dist Ct 2009).

Setoguchi v Uber, ABQB.

Shore v Avid Life Media Inc and Avid Dating Life Inc, ONSC.

Simpson v Facebook, Inc, ONSC File No CV-18-00597085-00CP.

Sofio c Organisme canadien de réglementation du commerce des valeurs mobilières (OCRCVM), 2015 QCCA 1820.

Sofio c Organisme canadien de réglementation du commerce des valeurs mobilières (OCRCVM), 2014 QCCS 4061.

Sorenson v Easyhome Ltd, 2013 ONSC 4017.

Spokeo, Inc v Robins, 136 S Ct 1540 (2016).

St-Jean v Mercier, [2002] 1 SCR 491, 209 DLR (4th) 513.

Steinman v CIBC, ONSC, CV-18-00599875-00, June 15, 2018.

Stevens v SNF Maritime Metal Inc, 2010 FC 1137.

Stuart Thiel and Brianna Thicke c Facebook Inc and Facebook Canada Ltd, QCSC.

Teck Cominco Metals Ltd v Lloyd's Underwriters, 2009 SCC 11.

The Fehmarn, [1958] 1 All E.R. 333.

TJX Companies Retail Sec Breach Litigation, 564 F (3d) 489 at 491 (1st Cir 2009).

Tolofson v Jensen, [1994] 3 SCR 1022 (SCC), 120 DLR (4th) 289.

Townsend v SunLife Financial, 2012 FC 550.

Tucci v Peoples Trust Company, 2017 BCSC 1525.

Tucci v Peoples Trust Company, 2015 BCSC 987.

Tucci v Peoples Trust, 2013 BCSC.

Union des Consommateurs c Bell, 2011 QCCS 1118.

Veilleux c Compagnie d'assurance-vie Penncorp, 2008 QCCA 257.

Vivendi Canada Inc v Dell'Aniello, 2014 SCC 1, [2014] 1 SCR 3.

Walter Energy Canada Holdings Inc (Re), [2017] BCJ No 820, 2017 BCSC 709.

Western Canadian Shopping Centres Inc v Dutton, 2001 SCC 46.

Wilson v Bank of Montreal, ONSC CV-18-00599876-00, filed on June 15, 2018.

Won Kil Bai v Marriott, QCSC.

Wong v Marriott, BCSC.

Wong v TJX Cos, 2008 CarswellOnt 523, 2008 CanLII 3421 (ONSC).

Z.I. Pompey Industrie v ECU-Line N.V, 2003 SCC 27.

Zuckerman v Target Corporation Inc, 2018 QCCS 5497.

Zuckerman v Target Corporation, 2017 QCCS 110.

Zuckerman v Target Corporation, 2016 QCCS 3160.

Zuckerman v Target Corp, 2015 QCCS 1285.

Books, articles, reports and other secondary material

Anupam, Chandler, Margot Kaminski & William McGeveran, "Catalyzing Privacy Law" [draft 2020].

Article 29 Data Protection Working Party, *Opinion 06/2014 on the notion of legitimate interests of the data controller under Article 7 of Directive 95/46/EC*, 844/14/EN WP 217.

Basedow, Jurgen et al, eds, *Max Planck Encyclopaedia of European Private Law*, (Oxford University Pres, December 2011).

Ben-Shahar, Omri & Ariel Porat, "The Restoration Remedy in Private Law" (2018) 118 Colum L Rev 1901.

Berryman, Jeff & Robyn Carroll, "Cy-Pres as a Class Action Remedy—Justly Maligned or Just Misunderstood?" in Kit Barker & Darryn Jensen, eds, *Private Law: Key Encounters with Public Law* (Cambridge: Cambridge University Press, 2013).

"Beyond Big Business: Contests between Jurisdictions in a Vertically Integrated Global Economy" (November 2000) LSUC, Civil Litigation Forum, Toronto.

Browne, Peter S, "Computer Security – A Survey" (1972) 4:3 SIGMIS Database 1.

Burns, Stephen D et al, "Breach Notification Rules Under GDPR, PIPEDA, and PIPA" (1 October 2018), online (blog): *Bennett Jones* <bennettjones.com/Blogs-Section/Breach-Notification-Rules-under-GDPR-PIPEDA-and-PIPA>.

Calo, Ryan, "The Boundaries of Privacy Harm" (2010) 86:3 Ind L J.

———, "People Can Be So Fake: A New Dimension to Privacy and Technology Scholarship" (2010) 114 Penn St L Rev 809.

Charney Lawyers, "Ashley Madison Class Action Lawsuit" online: *Charney Lawyers*.

Citron, Danielle Keats, "Mainstreaming Privacy Torts" (2010) 98 Cal L Rev 1805.

Cofone, Ignacio N, "Nothing to Hide, but Something to Lose" (2019) 70:1 UTLJ 64.

———, "Privacy Law Needs Privacy Harm" (30 August 2019), online: *The Hill* <thehill.com/opinion/cybersecurity/459427-privacy-law-needs-privacy-harm>.

———, "The Dynamic Effect of Information Privacy Law" (2017) 18:2 Minn J L Sci & Tech 517.

———, "A Healthy Amount of Privacy: Quantifying Privacy Concerns in Medicine" (2017) 65:1 Clev St L Rev 1.

——— & Adriana Z Robertson, "Privacy Harms" (2018) 69 Hastings LJ 1039.

Cohen, Asher A, "Settling Cy Pres Settlements: Analyzing the Use of Cy Pres Class Action Settlements" (2019) 32 Geo J Leg Ethics 451.

Complaint, *David Mutnick v Clearview AI, Inc*, No 1:20-cv-00512 (ND Ill Jan 22, 2020).

Compliance agreement between the Privacy Commissioner of Canada and Equifax Canada Co, (April 2019).

Convention of 2 July 2019 on the Recognition and Enforcement of Foreign Judgments in Civil or Commercial Matters, online: <www.hcch.net/en/instruments/conventions/full-text/?cid=137>.

Court of Justice of the European Union (September 2019) on the scope of the "right to be forgotten", online: <curia.europa.eu/jcms/upload/docs/application/pdf/2019-09/cp190112en.pdf>.

CTV News, "Nissan Canada informs financing customers of possible data breach" (December 21, 2017), online: *CTV News* <www.ctvnews.ca/autos/nissan-canada-informs-financing-customers-of-possible-data-breach-1.3731485>.

De Groot, Juliana, "The History of Data Breaches" (24 October 2019), online (blog): *Digital Guardian* <digitalguardian.com/blog/history-data-breaches>.

Delwaide, Karl &Antoine Aylwin, *Leçons tirées de dix ans d'expérience: la Loi sur la protection des renseignements personnels dans le secteur privé du Québec* (Ottawa: Commissaire à la protection de la vie privée du Canada, 2005).

Delwaide, Karl et al, *Learning from a Decade of Experience: Quebec's Private Sector Privacy Act* (Privacy Commissioner of Canada, 2005).

DLA Piper, "Germany: First Court Decision on Claims for Immaterial Damages under GDPR" (12 December 2018), online (blog): *Privacy Matters* <blogs.dlapiper.com/privacymatters/germany-first-court-decision-on-claims-for-immaterial-damages-under-gdpr/>.

Di Carlo, Carlo, "Invasions of Privacy: Class Proceedings" in Gerald Chan & Nader R Hasan, eds, *Digital Privacy: Criminal, Civil and Regulatory Litigation* (Toronto: LexisNexis, 2018).

Dicey, AV, *A Digest of the Law of England with reference to the Conflict of Laws* (London: Stevens & Sons, 1896).

DLA Piper, "Germany: First Court Decision on Claims for Immaterial Damages under GDPR" (12 December 2018), online (blog): *Privacy Matters* <blogs.dlapiper.com/privacymatters/germany-first-court-decision-on-claims-for-immaterial-damages-under-gdpr/>.

Douez v Facebook, 2017 SCC 33 (Factum of the Intervener, Canadian Civil Liberties Association).

Draba, Robert E, "Motorsports Merchandise: A Cy Pres Distribution Not Quite 'as Near as Possible'" (2004) 16:2 Loyola Consumer L Rev 121.

Equifax Data Breach Settlement, Federal Trade Commission (Jan 2020), online: <www.ftc.gov/enforcement/cases-proceedings/refunds/equifax-data-breach-settlement>.

"Factum of Intervener the Electronic Frontier Foundation", online: <www.scc-csc.ca/WebDocuments-DocumentsWeb/36602/FM090_Intervener_Electronic-Frontier_Foundation.pdf>.

Finn, Shaun E, *Class Actions in Québec: Notes for Non-Residents*, 2nd ed (Montréal: Thomson Reuters, 2018).

Gady, Franz-Stefan, "EU/U.S. Approaches to Data Privacy and the 'Brussels Effects': A Comparative Analysis" (2014) 15 Georgetown J of Intl Affairs 12.

Gavison, Ruth E, "Privacy and the Limits of Law" (1980) 89 Yale LJ 421.

Gemalto, "Breach Level Index" (2018), online: <breachlevelindex.com/>.

Glaspell, Barry, "The Increasing Settlement Costs of Mass Privacy Breaches" (2018) 13:2 Canadian Class Action Review 335.

Global News, "Ashley Madison parent company settles data breach lawsuit for $11.2 M", *Global News* (July 14, 2017).

Goodlander, John, "Cy Pres Settlements: Problems Associated with the Judiciary's Role and Suggested Solutions", Note, (2015) 56:2 Boston College L Rev 733.

Gratton, Eloïse, *Understanding Personal Information: Managing Privacy Risks* (Montreal: LexisNexis Canada, 2013).

———, "Section 1.1 The Historical Background Leading to Laws Protection Personal Information" in *Understanding Personal Information: Managing Privacy Risks* (Montreal: LexisNexis Canada, 2013).

———, "If Personal Information is Privacy's Gatekeeper, then Risk of Harm is the Key: A Proposed Method for Determining What Counts as Personal Information" (2013) 24:1 Alb L J Sci & Tech.

——— & Christopher C Maughan, "Superior Court of Québec Authorizes Privacy Class Action in Zuckerman v. Target Corporation", Case Comment (2017), online: *CanLII Connects* <www.canliiconnects.org/en/commentaries/44655>.

Ha-Redeye, Omar, "Class Action Intrusions: A Development in Privacy Rights or an Indeterminate Liability" (2015) 6 WJ Legal Stud 1.

Harris, Liam, "Understanding Public Policy Limits to the Enforceability of Forum Selection Clauses After *Douez v Facebook*" (2019) JPIL 50.

Hillebrand, Gail & Daniel Torrence, "Claims Procedures in Large Consumer Class Actions and Equitable Distribution of Benefits" (1988) 28 Santa Clara L Rev 747.

Hubley, Jessica L, "How Concepcion Killed the Privacy Class Action" (2011) 28:4 Santa Clara Comp & High Tech LJ 743.

IAPP-EY, *Annual Governance Report 2018* (2018).

IBM, "2018 Cost of a Data Breach Study: Global Overview" (2018), online: *IBM Security* <databreachcalculator.mybluemix.net/>.

Information and Privacy Commissioner, *Investigation into a Privacy Breach of Customers' Personal Information by the British Columbia Lottery Corporation (Re)*, (2011 BCIPC 6 (CanLII)).

Innovation, Science and Economic Development Canada, *Strengthening Privacy for the Digital Age, Proposals to Modernize the Personal Information Protection and Electronic Documents Act*, May 2019.

ISO/IEC 27000:2018, "Information technology – Security techniques – Information security management systems – Overview and vocabulary" (2018), online: *ISO* <www.iso.org/standard/73906.html>.

Joint investigation of Ashley Madison by the Privacy Commissioner of Canada and the Australian Privacy Commissioner/Acting Australian Information Commissioner, (CanLII 104108 (PCC), 2016).

Jois, Goutam U, "The Cy Pres Problem and the Role of Damages in Tort Law" (2008) 16 Va J Soc Pol'y & L 258.

Johnston, Jennifer, "Cy Pres Comme Possible to anything is Possible: How Cy Pres Creates Improper Incentives in Class Action Settlements" (2013) 9 JL Econ & Policy 277.

Jukier, Rosalie, "Canada's Legal Traditions: Sources of Unification, Diversification, or Inspiration?" (2018) 11 J Civ L Stud 75.

———, "The Impact of Legal Traditions on Quebec Procedural Law: Lessons from Quebec's New Code of Civil Procedure" (2015) 93 Can Bar Rev 211.

Justice Committee on Privacy, "Privacy and the Law", discussed in Home Office, Lord Chancellor's Office, Scottish Office (Chairman The Rt Hon, Kenneth Younger).

Jutras, Daniel, "Alternative Compensation Schemes from a Comparative Perspective" in Mauro Bussani & Anthony J Sebok, eds, *Comparative Tort Law: Global Perpectives* (Cheltenham, UK: Edward Elgar Publishing, 2015) 151.

———, "Cartographie de la Mixité: La Common Law et la Complétude du Droit Civil au Québec" (2009) 88 La Revue du Barreau Canadien 247.

Kalajdzic, Jasminka, *Class Actions in Canada: The Promise and Reality of Access to Justice* (Vancouver: UBC Press, 2019).

———, "The 'Illusion of Compensation': Cy Pres Distributions in Canadian Class Actions" (2013) 92:2 Can Bar Rev 173.

Kaufman, Jeffrey A, *Privacy Law in the Private Sector* (Toronto: Thomson Reuters Publishing, 2019).

Kennedy, Gerard, "Jurisdiction Motions and Access to Justice: An Ontario Tale" (2018) 55 Osgoode Hall LJ 79.

Krueger, George G & Judd A Serotta, "Money for Nothing" (June 2, 2008) *Legal Times*.

Leskin, Paige, "The 21 Scariest Data Breaches of 2018" (30 December 2018), online: *Business Insider* <www.businessinsider.com/data-hacks-breaches-biggest-of-2018-2018-12>.

Lewis, Kevin M, "UPDATE: Is Cy Pres A-OK? Supreme Court to Consider When Class Action Settlements Can Pay a Charity Instead of Class Members" (2019), online (pdf): *Congressional Research Service* <fas.org/sgp/crs/misc/LSB10131.pdf>.

Liptak, Adam, "Doling Out Other People's Money" (26 Nov 2007), online: *The New York Times* <www.nytimes.com/2007/11/26/washington/26bar.html>.

Lord Collins of Mapesbury & Jonathan Harris, eds, *Dicey, Morris and Collins on the Conflict of Laws,* 15th ed (London: Sweet & Maxwell, 2018).

Marrocco, Andrae J, Lyndsay Wasser & Mitch Koczerginski, "Data Protection and Cybersecurity in Canada" (2019) 39:1 Franchise LJ 81.

McIsaac, Barbara, Kris Klein & Shaun Brown, *Privacy Law in Canada* (Toronto: Thomson Reuters Publishing, 2018).

Merriam Webster, *Dictionary,* (2019) sub verbo "secure", online: www.merriam-webster.com/dictionary/secure.

Milano, Ashley, "Ashley Madison Class Action Plaintiffs Identify Themselves", *Top Class Actions* (June 18, 2016).

Ministère de la Justice, *A Plan to Modernise the Justice System*, March 2018, online (pdf): *Ministère de la Justice* <www.justice.gouv.qc.ca/fileadmin/user_upload/contenu/documents/En__Anglais_/centredoc/publications/ministere/dossiers/Justice_1819.pdf>.

Myhr, Peder, "Class-action lawsuit filed in Canada against Ashley Madison", *Global News* (August 20, 2015).

National Conference of State Legislatures, "Security Breach Notification Laws" (29 September 2019), online: *National Conference of State Legislatures* <www.ncsl.org/research/telecommunications-and-information-technology/security-breach-notification-laws.aspx>.

National Institute of Standards and Technology, *Computer Security Resource Center,* (last visited 2019) sub verbo "data", online: <csrc.nist.gov/glossary/term/data>.

National Institute of Standards and Technology, *Computer Security Resource Center*, (last visited 2019) sub verbo "information security", online <https://csrc.nist.gov/glossary/term/information-security>.

Naudie, Christopher & Evan Thomas, "Privacy Class Actions, by the numbers" (31 May 2017), online (blog): *Osler* <osler.com/en/blogs/classactions/may-2017/privacy-class-actions-by-the-numbers>.

Oates, Steven, "Caller ID: Privacy Protector or Privacy Invader" (1992) U Ill L Rev 219.

Office of the Information and Privacy Commissioner for British Columbia, *Investigation Report F06-01, Sale of Provincial Government Computer Tapes Containing Personal Information* (March 31, 2006).

Office of the Information and Privacy Commissioner of Alberta, *Breach Notification Decision P2018-ND-121* (FastHealth Corporation).

Office of the Information and Privacy Commissioner of Alberta, *Breach Notification Decision P2017-ND-145* (Sun Life Global Investments).

Office of the Information and Privacy Commissioner of Alberta, *Breach Notification Decision P2016-ND-12* (Function Point Productivity Software).

Office of the Information and Privacy Commissioner of Alberta, *Breach Notification Decision P2015-ND-80* (U.S. Fund for UNICEF).

Office of the Information and Privacy Commissioner of Alberta, *Breach Notification Decision P2013-ND-58* (C.S.T. Consultants Inc).

Office of the Information and Privacy Commissioner of Alberta, *Implementing Reasonable Safeguards, Personal Information Protection Act. Advisory #8.*

Office of the Information and Privacy Commissioner of Alberta, *Investigation Report #P2006-IR-003.*

Office of the Information and Privacy Commissioner of Alberta, *Investigation Report P2005-IR-006* (Report of an Investigation Concerning the Disclosure and Security of Personal Information, CBV Collection Services Ltd, July 21, 2005).

Office of the Privacy Commissioner of Canada, *Incident Summary #5 – Life insurance company employs best practices in responding to mass mailing error that risked exposing personal information.*

Office of the Privacy Commissioner of Canada & the Office of the Information and Privacy Commissioner of Alberta, *Report of an Investigation into the Security, Collection and Retention of Personal Information, PIPEDA Report of Findings #2007-389*, TJX Companies Inc. / Winners Merchant International LP (September 25 2007).

Office of the Privacy Commissioner of Canada & Office of the Information and Privacy Commissioner of Alberta, *Report of an Investigation into the Security, Collection and Retention of Personal Information*, (CanLII 41283 (PCC), 2007).

Office of the Privacy Commissioner of Canada, *PIPEDA Case Summary #2008-395*, Safeguards complaint against CIBC (January 2008).

Office of the Privacy Commissioner of Canada, *PIPEDA Case Summary #2007-377* (2007).

Office of the Privacy Commissioner of Canada, *PIPEDA Case Summary #2006-356* (2006).

Office of the Privacy Commissioner of Canada, *PIPEDA Case Summary #2003-180* (2003).

Office of the Privacy Commissioner of Canada, *PIPEDA Case Summary #2003-128* (2003).

Office of the Privacy Commissioner of Canada, *PIPEDA Case Summary #2002-177* (2002).

Office of the Privacy Commissioner of Canada, *PIPEDA Case Summary #2002-72* (2002).

Office of the Privacy Commissioner of Canada, *PIPEDA Case Summary #2001-5* (2001).

Office of the Privacy Commissioner of Canada, *PIPEDA Report of Findings #2019-001*, Investigation into Equifax Inc. and Equifax Canada Co.'s compliance with PIPEDA in light of the 2017 breach of personal information (April 9, 2019).

Office of the Privacy Commissioner of Canada, *PIPEDA Report of Findings #2015-001* (2015).

Office of the Privacy Commissioner of Canada, *PIPEDA Report of Findings #2014-003* (2014).

Office of the Privacy Commissioner of Canada, *PIPEDA Report of Findings #2012-009* (2012).

Office of the Privacy Commissioner of Canada, "What you need to know about mandatory reporting of breaches of security safeguards", online: *Office of the Privacy Commissioner of Canada* <www.priv.gc.ca/en/privacy-topics/privacy-breaches/respond-to-a-privacy-breach-at-your-business/gd_pb_201810/>.

Ormerod, Peter C, "A Private Enforcement Remedy for Information Misuse" (2019) 60:7 Boston College L Rev 1893.

"Personal information and data protection", online: *Mouvement Desjardins* <www.desjardins.com/ca/personal-information/index.jsp>.

Piché, Catherine, "Class Action Value" (2018) 19:1 Theoretical Inquiries L 261.

——— & Genevieve Saumier, "Consumer Collective Redress in Canada" (2018) 61 Japanese YB Int'l L 231.

Pomerantz, Abraham L, "New Developments in Class Actions – Has Their Death Knell Been Sounded" (1969) 25:3 Bus Lawyer 1259.

Power, Michael, *The Law of Privacy*, 2nd ed (Toronto: LexisNexis, 2017).

Prosser, William L, "Privacy" (1960) 48 Cal L Rev 383.

Redish, Martin H et al, "Cy Pres Relief and the Pathologies of the Modern Class Action: A Normative and Empirical Analysis" (2010) 62 Fla L Rev 617.

"Registry of Class Actions", online: *Registre des actions collectives* <www.registre desactionscollectives.quebec/en>.

Report of the Committee on Privacy, (presented to Parliament by the Secretary of State for the Home Department, the Lord High Chancellor and the Secretary of State for Scotland by Command of Her Majesty, July 1972).

Rodríguez Diez, Javier Esteban & María Elisa Zavala Achurra, "Restitución e Indemnización a Sujetos Indeterminados, Cy-Près y Acciones de Clase" (2019) 21 Estudios Socio-Jurídicos 151.

Rotenberg, Marc & David Jacobs, "Enforcing Privacy Rights: Class Action Litigation and the Challenge of Cy Pres" in David Wright & Paul De Hert, eds,

Enforcing Privacy: Regulatory, Legal and Technological Approaches (Switzerland, Springer: 2016) 307.

Safayeni, Justin, "Invasions of Privacy: Civil and Regulatory Consequences" in Gerald Chan & Nader R Hasan, eds, *Digital Privacy: Criminal, Civil and Regulatory Litigation* (Toronto: LexisNexis, 2018).

Saint Louis, Catherine, "Cellphones Test Strength of Gym Rules", *New York Times* (December 7, 2011).

Saunders, John & Paul Waldie, "Human error caused massive RBC glitch, officials concedes", (10 June 2004, last updated 20 April 2018), online: *The Globe and Mail* <www.theglobeandmail.com/report-on-business/human-error-caused-massive-rbc-glitch-official-concedes/article1000439/>.

Scassa, Teresa, "PIPEDA reform should include a comprehensive rewrite" (July 9, 2018), online (blog): *Teresa Scassa* <www.teresascassa.ca/index.php?option=com_k2&view=item&id=279:pipeda-reform-should-include-a-comprehensive-rewrite&Itemid=80>.

Segall, Laurie, "Pastor outed on Ashley Madison commits suicide", *CNN Business* (September 8, 2015).

Shepherd, Stewart R, "Comment, Damage Distribution in Class Actions: The Cy Pres Remedy" (1972) 39 U Chicago L Rev 448.

Shiel, Cecily C, "A New Generation of Class Action Cy Pres Remedies: Lessons from Washington State Notes & Comments" (2015) 90 Wash L Rev 943.

Skinner-Thomson, Scott, "Privacy's Double Standard" (2018) 93:4 Wash L Rev 2051.

Slobom, Michael J, "Recalibrating Cy Pres Settlements to Restore the Equilibrium" (2018) 123 Dick L Rev 281.

Solove, Daniel J & Paul M Schwartz, *Privacy Law Fundamentals*, 5th ed (Portsmouth, NH: IAPP, 2019).

Solove, Daniel J & Danielle Keats Citron, "Risk and Anxiety: A Theory of Data-Breach Harms" (2018) 96 Texas L Rev 737.

Spindler/Horváth, "DS-GVO Art. 82 - Haftung und Recht auf Schadenersatz" in Spindler/Schuster, *Recht der elektronischen Medien*, 4th ed (Munich: CHBeck, 2019).

Tene, Omer & Jules Polonetsky, "A Theory of Creepy: Technology, Privacy and Shifting Social Norms" (2013) 16 Yale JL & Tech 59.

Tennyson, Lord Alfred, *Aylmer's Field,* 1793.

Trakman, Leon, Robert Walters & Bruno Zeller, "Tort and Data Protection Law: Are There Any Lessons to be Learnt?" (2019) 5:4 European Data Protection L Rev 500.

Treasury Board Secretariat, "Notification to Affected Individuals: Sample Letter".

Trivisonno, Chris, "Developing a Consistent Approach to Balance Distributions in Quebec" (2016) 11 Can Class Action Rev 321.

Walker, Janet, "Specialised International Courts, Keeping Arbitration on top of its Game" (2019) 85 Arbitration 1.

———, "Class Actions Come of Age in Ontario" in Catherine Piché, ed, *The Class Action Effect: From the Legislator's Imagination to Today's Uses and Practices* (Éditions Yvon Blais, 2018).

————— et al, *Class Actions in Canada: Cases, Notes, and Materials*, 2nd ed (Toronto: Emond Publishing, 2018).

—————, "*Teck Cominco* and the wisdom of deferring to the court first seised, all things being equal" (2009) 47 CBLJ 192.

—————, "Castillo v Castillo: Closing the Barn Door" (2006) 43 Cdn Bus LJ 487.

—————, *Canadian Conflict of Laws,* 6 ed (LexisNexis, 2005+), c 3.6.

Varuhas, Jason & NA Moreham, *Remedies for Breach of Privacy* (London: Hart Publishing, 2018).

Vermeys, Nicolas, "Fostering Trust and Confidence in Electronic Commerce: Will the EU-Canada Comprehensive Economic and Trade Agreement Really Effect Change?" (2015) 20:2 *Lex Electronica* 63.

—————, *Responsabilité civile et sécurité informationnelle*, (Cowansville, QC: Yvon Blais, 2010).

————— & Emmanuelle Amar, with the collaboration of Vincent Gautrais, "Le dépôt technologique des documents" (2016) study presented to the Ministère de la Justice du Québec.

Vijayan, Jaikumar, "TJX data breach: At 45.6M card numbers, it's the biggest ever" (29 March 2007), online: *Computerworld* <www.computerworld.com/article/2544306/tjx-data-breach–at-45-6m-card-numbers–it-s-the-biggest-ever.html>.

Warren, Samuel D & Louis D Brandeis, "The Right to Privacy" (1890) 4:5 Harv L Rev 193.

Westin, Alan F, *Privacy and Freedom* (New York: Atheneum Press, 1967).

Whitman, James Q, "The Two Western Cultures of Privacy: Dignity versus Liberty" (2004) 113:6 Yale LJ 1152.

Winkler, Warren K et al, The Law of Class Actions in Canada (Toronto: Thomson Reuters, 2014).

Yospe, Sam, "Cy Pres Distributions in Class Action Settlements", Note, (2009) 2009:3 Colum Bus L Rev 1014.

Zanfir-Fortuna, Gabriela, "Article 82" in Christopher Kuner, Lee A Bygrave & Christopher Docksey, eds, *The EU General Data Protection Regulation: A Commentary* (Oxford University Press, 2020).

Index

access to information 20–23, 89, 94
Act to Establish a Legal Framework for
Information Technology 7, 85
appeal 14, 53, 93, 100, 102–103;
see also Court of Appeals
A.T. v Globe24h.com 47
award/awarded 3, 12–13, 27, 47, 55,
91, 93–94, 101–103, 108–109,
111–112; see also damages awards

bargaining power 59, 64–66, 67
BC Personal Information Protection
Act (PIPA) 68–70
BC Privacy Act 57–58, 76–77
BC privacy rights 75–78
Belley 24
Bourbonnière v. Yahoo! Inc. 53
Brandeis, Louis D. 25, 42, 44
breaches 1–2; see also security breach
British Columbia 6, 8, 21, 31, 33,
57–58, 65–66, 73, 75–78
British Columbia Workers
Compensation Board 65
Brown, Peter S. 83–84
business models 6

California 58, 66
California Consumer Privacy Act 7
Calo, Ryan 44, 47
cameras 42
Canada 1–8, 13–14, 20, 26, 32, 34, 44,
64, 70, 73, 80, 110–112
causality 12, 91, 94–96
certification 4, 5, 10, 14–15, 16, 20,
22, 29

Charter of Human Rights and Freedoms
19, 31; Choice of Court 63
Citron, Danielle K. 28–29
Civil Code; of California 4n15; of
Dutch 9; of Québec (CCQ) 8, 19, 30,
50, 61, 63, 70
civil litigation 1, 9, 78, 111
class action: advantages of 17–18;
application of 18–24; cause of 15,
24–25; commonality 16, 25–27;
defined 14–16; legislation 15–17;
preferability 16–17; representation
27–28; types of 32; see also privacy
class actions
class members 5, 12, 14, 16–17, 20, 24,
26, 39, 47, 52, 91, 99–106, 108–110
class proceedings 4–6
Communications Decency Act 76
Complaint 6n33, 35, 38n34, 59, 103
compliance agreements/class action
settlements 51
Condon v Canada 21–22, 52, 92
confidentiality 84, 85, 86
confidentiality integrity, and
availability (CIA) 84
contract 3, 22, 37, 58–60, 71, 75, 77;
consumer contracts 60–64
consumers: safeguarding rights of
62–64; transactions 62–63; rights
62–64
Court Jurisdiction and Proceedings
Transfer Act (CJPTA) 62–63
Court of Appeals 11, 19, 21–22, 30, 44,
58, 103
customer information, sensitive 81

cybersecurity 2n3, 4, 7, 7n40, 81, 82
cy près comme possible 99
cy près settlements 99–112; in bijural
   Canada 109–112; challenges of
   107–109; *Frank v Gaos* 101–105;
   overview 99–101; usefulness
   105–107

damages 43–53, 92–94; overview
   30–33; privacy wrongdoing 33–43
damages awards 19, 46, 106
data breach 7, 28, 36–37, 39, 51,
   53–54, 81–82, 86, 90–91, 95
data protection 1–2, 6–7, 9–11
data protection law 33–35, 37–39,
   41–43; British data protection law 9;
   Canadian Data Protection Laws 35;
   draft 33
data security: breaches 8, 95; incidents
   35–39
de novo application 3, 6
device 4, 11, 20–21, 26, 32; drugs or
   medical 25; mobile; 45; physical
   memory device 21–22
Dicey, A.V. 61, 79
Digital Privacy Act 88
Douez v Facebook 26, 56–80;
   challenges of 64–67; consumer
   contracts 60–64; limits of comity
   73–78; mandatory law 67–73;
   missed opportunities 58–60;
   Morguard in post-territorial
   world 78–80; overview 56–57;
   quasi-constitutional rights 67–73;
   sponsored stories 57–60
Drew v Walmart Canada Inc. 52

electronic communication service 102
Eleftheria/Pompey 59, 66
employee access 11, 22–24, 28
encrypted/encryption 24, 38, 92;
   see also unencrypted
enforcement 2, 7, 11, 14, 29, 69, 71, 74,
   79, 106
Equifax 22, 31n7, 37, 49–51;
   2017 Equifax data breach 37,
   105–106
Europe 70, 87
European Union 9, 62
Evans v The Bank of Nova Scotia 52

Facebook 26, 95, 57
Fair Information Practices 34
Federal Court of Appeal 22
Federal Trade Commission 79, 106
First Amendment 76, 79
forum selection 58, 60, 63, 67–69,
   76–78
Frank v Gaos 101–105

Gavison, Ruth E. 44
General Data Protection Regulation
   (GDPR) 6–7, 9, 40
*Girao v Zarek Taylor Grossman
   Hanrahan LLP* 47
Google 76, 80, 95, 101–102

hacker-based claims 5–6
hackers 21–22
Hague Convention on the
   Recognition 79
harm: objective 47–53; privacy 18;
   subjective 43–47; type of 46
health information 11, 21, 23, 24, 26,
   45, 83
Health Information Privacy And
   Management Act, Yukon
   Territory 83
*Hemeon v South West Nova District
   Health Authority* 47
Hollick v Toronto (City) 17
Home Depot 39, 95
Hopkins v Kay 21, 22
House of Lords 65
Human rights 19, 19n38, 31, 31n4, 75

identity 20, 24–25, 28, 43, 46, 48–49,
   51–52, 54–55, 91–93, 95
Illinois, Biometric Information Privacy
   Act 6
inequality 59, 64–66
information: security 83–86; sensitive
   40, 45, 81, 94
Information Technology Act 85, 89
integrity 85–86
Internet 13; communications 60;
   service provider 45; streaming media
   40; traffic 45

Jones v. Tsige 3–4, 19, 24, 30, 44
judicial approval 14–15

jurisdiction 2, 3, 5, 9–11, 14–15, 34,
37, 57–68, 71, 74–78, 110
Jutras, Daniel 107n34, 111n66

Kalajdzic, Jasminka 5n22, 25n69,
27n85, 111n65, 111n68, 111n70
Kochar v University of Saskatchewan
89–90

Lacoursière, J. 24–25
Ladas v Apple Inc. 26
legal pathways 6–9
legislation 1, 4, 15–17, 33, 37, 68, 70,
76–77, 81, 83–87, 90, 91
Lozanski v The Home Depot, Inc. 39, 52

mandatory law 67–73
mandatory rules: and questions of
procedure 72–73; *vs.* public policy
70–72
Manitoba 8, 31, 70–71
Mazzonna 24
McLachlin, C. J. 17
Moran v Pyle 64
Morguard in post-territorial world 78–80
Mustapha v Culligan of Canada Ltd 93

negative jurisdiction 63–64
Newfoundland and Labrador 8, 31
Nova Scotia community hospital 47
Notice 15, 31n7, 87, 106

objective harm 47–53
online web service provider 45
opt-in 40–41
opt-out 40, 101, 110
Ontario 3–4, 8, 21, 65, 70
Ontario Class Proceedings Act, 1992
(CPA) 15
Ontario Court of Appeal 19, 21, 30, 44
Ontario Superior Court 19
Organisation for Economic
Co-operation and Development
(OECD) 33
Ottawa 57–58

Payment Card Industry Data Security
Standard 38
Personal Health Information Protection
Act (PHIPA) 21

personal data 7n40, 30n1, 50, 90
personal information 35–41; access
20, 22; adequate security measures
34; of citizens and consumer
1; collection, processing, and
dissemination of 4; collection, use,
and disclosure of 13; collection of
23, 44; confidentiality of 36, 84; data
subject's health 20; defined 83–84;
electronically stored 21; failure
to protect 31; impact of security
breaches on 12; inherent economic
value of 19; loss of physical memory
device 20; mismanagement of 11;
security breach 37; sensitivity of 88;
theft of 32; unauthorized sale of 23
Personal Information Protection Act
(PIPA), Alberta 87, 89
Personal Information Protection and
Electronic Documents Act (PIPEDA)
2–3, 6–7, 18–19, 33–35, 38, 40–42,
46, 48–50, 83, 88, 89
photography 42
Piché, Catherine 101n7, 111n69
PIPEDA Safeguards Principle 48–50
Pompey 59
preferability 16–17, 18, 24, 74
Privacy Act 6, 6n31, 6n36, 7, 8n44, 19,
26, 31n5, 49n106, 57–58, 68–69,
75–77, 88
privacy: harm 18; tort 6, 8; training
36; violations 1, 3–4, 8, 30, 98;
wrongdoing 33–43
privacy class actions: categorization
31–32; challenges of 64–67;
changing times 64–67; classification
5–6; class proceedings 4–6;
cross-border claims 5; described
1–2; in digital era 66–67;
importance of 2–4; legal pathways
6–9; multijurisdictional issues 5;
private rights of 2–3; role of 1;
uncertainties and lessons learned
30–55; unfulfilled promise 13–30;
widespread accessibility of 28–29;
widespread use of 23–29; *see also*
class action
privacy commissioner: of Alberta 81;
Office of the Privacy Commissioner
of Canada (OPC) 2–3, 6, 33,

35–38, 40, 48, 50–51, 81; Privacy Commissioner of Canada 81, 91
privacy law *see* class action; privacy class actions
private law 5, 11, 13, 14, 18, 25, 71n52, 104n26, 111n67
Proceedings 15, 17, 23, 47, 62, 73–75, 91; administrative 20; civil 20; class proceedings 4–5, 15, 15n8; divorce 47; foreign 74; parallel 73–75
Prosser, William L. 44

quasi-constitutional 59, 67–73, 75
Québec 4, 6–8, 14, 17, 19, 24, 33, 82
Québec Charter of Human Rights and Freedoms 31
Québec Civil Code (CCQ) 94–96
Québec Superior Court 53

reasonable expectations 40–41
Registry of Class Actions, Québec 82
relief 12, 13, 101–104, 108
remedy 2, 5, 10, 13, 52, 80, 99n3, 104n26, 105n27, 111n67
Report of Findings 36–38, 40, 49
Roberts, John 103
Robertson, Adriana Z. 28–29
Rouyn Noranda, Québec 24
Rowlands v Durham Region Health 21–22
Rumley v British Columbia 17

Saskatchewan 8, 31, 65
Secure Sockets Layer (SSL) 38
security breach 6–8; as legal construct 83–90; liability 96–98; limits of notification legislation 86–90; overview 81–82; as premise for class action suits 90–98

sensitive information 40, 45, 81, 94
social media 13, 60
social norms 41
Sofio v Investment Industry Regulatory Organization of Canada 22, 53
Solove, Daniel J. 28–29
Spokeo, Inc. v. Robins 104
Stored Communications Act 102
subjective harm 43–47
Supreme court: British Columbia Supreme Court 22, 58; Canada Supreme Court 13, 17, 56, 58, 60, 64, 72–73; UK Supreme Court 65; US Supreme Court 27, 103

Teck Cominco 73–74
Tolofson v Jensen 72
tort law 1–2, 8–9, 32, 107, 107n34, 107n36
Treasury Board Secretariat of Canada 51
Tucci v Peoples Trust Company 22

unencrypted 21, 22, 38, 45, 52
United States 1, 8, 24, 27, 73, 87
Use of Consumer Identification Information Act, Washington, D.C. 6

violations 1, 2, 3–4, 6, 8, 30, 98
Vivendi Canada Inc. v. Dell'Aniello 46

Warren, Samuel D. 25, 42, 44
Washington, D.C., Use of Consumer Identification Information Act 6
Western Canadian Shopping Centres Inc. v Dutton 17
website 47, 80, 101–102
Wi-Fi 38, 45

Yukon Territory, Health Information Privacy And Management Act 83

For Product Safety Concerns and Information please contact our EU
representative GPSR@taylorandfrancis.com
Taylor & Francis Verlag GmbH, Kaufingerstraße 24, 80331 München, Germany

www.ingramcontent.com/pod-product-compliance
Lightning Source LLC
Chambersburg PA
CBHW061329220326
41599CB00026B/5096